The Retail Sales Bible

❧

The GREAT Book of G.R.E.A.T. Selling!

BY RICK SEGEL, CSP
AND
MATTHEW HUDSON, PhD

SPECIFIC HOUSE PUBLISHING
ORLANDO AND BOSTON

Published by
Specific House Publishing
268 Hamrick Drive
Kissimmee, FL 34759

Requests for permission should be sent to:
Specific House Publishing
268 Hamrick Drive
Kissimmee, FL 34759
781-272-9995
800-814-7998
rick@ricksegel.com / www.ricksegel.com

Printed in the United States of America
ISBN 978-1-934683-04-0

*Cover and text design by Julia Gignoux, Freedom Hill Book Design and
Production House*

CONTENTS

ACKNOWLEDGMENTS

I would like to thank Matthew Hudson for his contributions to this book and for the patience he demonstrated during this challenging and transitional time period of my life.

I would like to thank Julia Gignoux for her work on the design of this book. To the team of Susan Reid, Maxene Rosenthal, and Michelle Singer who really don't know each other but worked together editing, proofing, rewriting, and editing some more to make this work into a user-friendly and go-to guide of retail selling.

I want to thank my family and especially my wife Margie, who has been the driving force behind this book from the very beginning. She is a partner in life and business. We have shared the birth of our children, grandchildren and 13 other books and have watched them all find a place in this world.

Lastly, I need to thank my audiences and readers for guiding me through and making this book what it is today. Keep those cards, e-mails, and letters coming, they make a difference.

Rick Segel, rick@ricksegel.com

WHAT'S
THE GREAT BOOK
OF G.R.E.A.T. SELLING
ALL ABOUT?

*The Retail Sales Bible: The GREAT Book of G.R.E.A.T.
Selling* is designed to be *the* ultimate authority, the indispensable resource and how-to-sell-better guide for professional salespeople. If you have a question about how to talk to customers, how to get customers to talk to you, the best way to present merchandise to customers, or how to sell more, you'll find the answers here!

"What's In It for Me?"

We're glad you asked that question! It's a GREAT sales question!

In fact, "What's in it for me?" is the pivotal question that makes retail happen. You see, that's the question your customers are asking each and every time they step into the store, each and every time you show them a piece of merchandise, each and every time they read a sign or view a display. They want to know what benefit they're going to receive if they give you their money.

After reading this book and learning the G.R.E.A.T. Selling System, you will:

Make More Sales

Make More Add-On Sales

Better Understand How People Buy

Be Able to Deal with Even the Most Difficult Customers

Have Much More Confidence

Master the Five Stages of the G.R.E.A.T. System of Selling

Know How to Make Customers Return Again and Again

Let's start this book off with a little note of reality — just to set the tone. Right now, chances are you've been given this book by your employer, who wants you to read it as part of your training. Or, you've picked it up on your own, looking for ways to do your job better.

Either way, you'll be happy to know that what you're going to read in these pages will help you become a more effective, more efficient salesperson. You're going to learn the techniques top sales professionals consistently use to form strong, ongoing relationships with customers, and how they leverage those relationships so that customers buy, buy, buy! So what's in it for you?

It Will Make Your Job Easier

The G.R.E.A.T. Selling technique will make your job much easier. By having a consistent strategy to implement with each and every customer, you won't have to reinvent the wheel!

The beauty of the G.R.E.A.T. Selling technique is that it is infinitely flexible. You can tweak it and adapt it so it best suits your store and your customers. But we promise you this: as long as you use all five phases, it is going to work!

Using the G.R.E.A.T. Selling technique also eliminates a lot of headache and stress. You'll be able to rely upon a proven methodology to connect with customers, concentrate on perfecting your performance, and enjoy better results. The hard work of discovering what works has already been done for you!

You'll be Happier

The techniques you'll learn here will give you two more reasons to be happy.

1. You truly will be helping people — your customers — meet their wants and fulill their needs

Using the G.R.E.A.T. Selling technique, you'll be able to help customers be truly satisfied with their purchases. **This is a big deal!** Think about it. Customers who shop on-line are forced to rely upon their own judgment and maybe web reviews from people they don't know. The vast majority of retail stores rely upon a self-serve concept as well. Customers can't find help if they stand on top of a product display, waving their arms, tooting a bugle, and wearing a sign that says "Helloooo! I'm here! I'm here to buy! Won't someone please, please help me?"

You, on the other hand, will be different. You will not only physically be there to help your customers, you'll actually listen to them, discover their needs and wants, provide education, and make suggestions that will enable them to have what they want, thus fulfilling their need.

This is so rare that it is staggering! You have an almost unique opportunity to help people and make a real difference in their lives.

2. You'll have more commissions and more job security

Picture this: Uncle Bob's General Store has three employees.

First, there's Bonnie. Bonnie does a great job every day. Her sales numbers are the highest, she sells the highest margin merchandise, and she has a lot of customers who love her.

The next salesperson — Bill — is what we call an average salesperson. He sells a fair amount of merchandise and is generally cheerful. No one ever asks for Bill by name, though, and his numbers aren't as high as Bonnie's.

Finally, we've got Beth. Poor Beth! She really hates working retail, and it shows. She shows up to work every day with a sour attitude. Customers who need help have to seek Beth out, because she's surely not coming to find them! Even then, she's not terribly helpful. More than a few customers have decided they're never going to shop at Uncle Bob's again if they see Beth is working.

In an environment where good jobs are hard to come by, **this is a very big deal**. When the economy goes down, most employers find they absolutely, positively have to cut costs. Employees are expensive. So if you're a below average or even average performer, you're in a prime position to lose your job. But if you're a GREAT salesperson, one who consistently sells a lot of merchandise and creates happy customers, you'll be sitting pretty — while everyone else is sweating bullets!

If You Manage People

Rest assured there are benefits in *The GREAT Book of G.R.E.A.T. Selling* for you, as well.

First and foremost, *The GREAT Book of G.R.E.A.T. Selling* will make life easy for you. Having one system that your entire team is following makes life infinitely easier. Everyone's sharing a common language, which makes training, motivating and rewarding your team a cinch.

Second, a rising tide lifts all the boats. When your people do better, you do better. Increased sales numbers will make a difference, not only in your compensation package, but in how you're viewed by your company. When you're the leader who makes a difference, you're the leader who gets recognized, promoted, and valued.

How to Use This Book

This book is designed for the working sales professional. We know you're too busy to sit down and read this cover to cover in one sitting. It's designed so you can open it to pretty much any page and find something you can use to improve your sales performance right away.

That being said, you'll get maximum benefit if you begin at the beginning and work through the pages and chapters in order. Each section builds on the section before, allowing you to draw on what you've already learned to make each new technique even more powerful.

A Note from the Authors

Neither of us is particularly boring in person, and we didn't want to write a boring book! That's why we decided to create Uncle Bob's General Store to use as our example. Rather than limit ourselves to one kind of store and bore (or alienate) those of you who don't work in that particular kind of store, Uncle Bob's General Store carries everything imaginable! Uncle Bob sells fine jewelry and ammunition, furniture and bridal gowns, lawn tractors and taxidermy supplies. You name it, he's got it!

Realistically, most of you don't work for Uncle Bob. Chances are you work for a specialty retailer or in a specialty department of a large retailer. But the techniques Uncle Bob uses work to sell everything he sells — and they're going to work for you, too!

Three sales people work for Uncle Bob: Bonnie, Bill, and Beth. What's with all the B's, you ask? We have no idea. Uncle Bob's weird that way.

But when you see a story featuring Uncle Bob, Bonnie, Bill, or Beth, you can "B" sure that their examples are going to work for you. Because our examples represent every kind of store, their wisdom will apply to your store. Oh, by the way, Beth, Bill and Bonnie recently finished reading *The GREAT Book of G.R.E.A.T. Selling*. So Beth's no longer a bad example and Bill's no longer average. All three have become GREAT salespeople. And you can, too!

Finally, sometimes we just can't help ourselves. There's just too much good information we want to share — GREAT ideas — that we can't bear to leave any out. So we didn't. You'll see throughout stuff that didn't "exactly" fit the chapter topic, but was too good to ignore, under the heading:

a random GREAT *idea*

And every now and then, just because we couldn't control ourselves, you'll see this:

another random GREAT *idea*

For example:

a random GREAT *idea*

Write in this book!

UNDERLINE! Circle those words and sentences that stand out! Make notes! Write down your thoughts in the margins! Highlight! Read this book inside and out! Make it work for you! Use sticky notes and bookmarks!

another random GREAT *idea*

If you've got a question that we haven't answered, e-mail me: rick@ricksegel.com.

Not only will we write you back, we'll use your GREAT question to make our next book even better!

Finally, this is one book, by two authors. Working together, we've tried to fill it with content that will be useful to the most sales professionals possible, no matter what type of store they work in.

We agree on most things, but not everything. So every now and then you'll see a little note that says *"Rick says..."* Matthew is the "book smart" side of the equation, with a Ph.D. as well as 25 years of retail experience. Rick, also a 25-year retail veteran, now a professional speaker, trainer and author, provides the "street smart" side of the equation. Between the two of us, we offer two (sometimes) different perspectives, and a wide range of information to help you handle almost any sales situation.

We hope you find *The Retail Sales Bible* a GREAT resource for real results!

Happy reading — and happy selling!

Matthew Hudson   Rick Segel

Chapter 1

WHAT ARE YOU REALLY SELLING?

"Service is selling and selling is service."

Ilearned that lesson from someone I never expected to learn any lesson from. A number of years ago I had a training job working with all of the Texaco and Shell dealers in New England and New York. When I first got started, I needed to be trained to know what it was like working at a gas station and convenience store. I worked at three different stations that knew that I was there to observe their actions and habits.

The next phase was to work at three stations that did not know I was a trainer and developer. I was assigned to work at this one particular station in Rhode Island and report to Ralph, the Assistant to the Assistant Manager. Ralph was one of the nicest human beings I had ever met. He was hard working and took his job very seriously. He had worked at this station for 11 years. His career goal was to work hard to eventually become the Assistant Manager. Many people would look at Ralph and consider him slow, but a better worker I don't think you could ever find.

The station was busy from the moment I got there. All I kept hearing Ralph say to every customer was "Don't forget to buy your lottery tickets. It's up to 42 million dollars tonight." Customer after customer, he would say, "Don't forget the lottery tickets!" or "You could be a millionaire!" or "We want to have a winner from this station!" This went on and on for almost two hours, until there was a break in the action and I turned to Ralph and said to him, "Ralph, you're a great salesman!" When I said that his face turned bright red, the veins in his neck popped out, and in a firm, harsh voice he said, "I am not a salesman type. I was just taking care of my customers!"

> *When we are selling a customer we are really servicing them, and when we service well we are really selling.*

The thing that was so powerful about Ralph was that he not only sold a lot of tickets, but every single customer thanked him. Great salespeople never feel like they are selling, because it feels natural and they are helping the customer, not "selling" the customer.

Does the best salesperson always make the sale?

Does the best store always sell to every customer?

Does the best politician always get elected?

Does the best person always get the job?

The answer to each of these questions is "NO!"

Generally, the winner always seems to be the one who we like. Buyers will go to trade shows and will walk by booths of businesses that have great products, deliver on time and have terrific prices, but they don't do business with them. Why?

Because they don't like them! I have actually talked to buyers who feel guilty because they're not making rational decisions.

They are right, their decision-making is not rational. They are truly predictably irrational. *Predictably Irrational* is the title of a best-selling book by Dan Ariely, a behavioral economist.

The Four Things You Must Sell

What are the four things you are selling when a customer walks into your store?

1. YOURSELF If they don't like you, it's an uphill battle.

2. THE STORE Does your ambiance create a sense of belonging?

3. THE EXPERIENCE How are you making them feel at that moment?

4. THE MERCHANDISE Notice that merchandise is actually last on the list!

1: YOURSELF

Yes, we're talking about you! First and foremost, the customer has to like the sales professional they're dealing with. They have to believe in you and feel that they can trust you to help them find the merchandise they want — and have fun doing it! This is easier if there's some kind of affinity between you and your customer. Common points of interest, sense of style, values or experiences can all serve to form a bond. Customers feel more comfortable when they're shopping in a store where they feel at ease with the sales staff. That's why it's critical to look approachable and be friendly.

A word of caution: If you badmouth your boss or your business, you will make your customer uncomfortable. People say not to take it personally. Wrong! It is all personal! And you — and your attitude — are an integral part of the sale.

In short, your customer has to like you in order to do business with you!

2: THE STORE

Customers will judge a store's appearance, layout, organization, decoration, cleanliness and more in a matter of seconds. Invisible factors like sound and smell have a huge impact on a customer's decision to stay and shop or to head back out the door.

The most important aspect of the store is the atmosphere, the ambiance — what a lot of people call the "feel" of the store. Think about your favorite store. Chances are there's something about the store that makes you feel comfortable and at ease while you're there. You feel like you belong. That sense of belonging is very important to most customers.

Cleanliness and organization are two factors that have a huge impact on a customer's decision to buy. A store should be designed with the customer's comfort in mind; otherwise, they're not going to stay!

3: THE EXPERIENCE

If the customer likes you and likes how the store looks, sounds, smells, and "feels," the next thing they consider is the experience they're having. This is a hard-to-define yet vital step. Customers want to **have fun** while they're shopping.

Let us let you in on one of the secrets of the retail world. It used to be, back in the dark ages when we were born (*Ahem! You mean when Rick was born ~ Matthew*), that retailers who provided good merchandise at good prices with good service would be in great shape.

That's not enough anymore. Good merchandise, good prices, and even good service are all taken for granted. They are expected. Stores must provide those things or they go right out of business. Customers have too many choices to put up with bad service!

Today's customers want something more. They want to have fun. They want to be entertained. They want to enjoy shopping. They want to learn. They want to socialize. Shopping has become about so much more than picking out merchandise.

Shopping is all about **the experience** customers have while picking out merchandise.

If your customers are having fun — or if they perceive that they're likely to have fun in your store — they're buying into the experience. If not, you've lost them.

4: THE MERCHANDISE

This is the last item the customer has to buy — the actual merchandise.

Did you get that? We're at number four — on a four-item list! The merchandise is the **last** thing the customer has to buy. They won't buy the merchandise if they haven't bought the three previous items!

It's only after the customer has decided that they like and want to do business with you, in your store, enjoying the experience you provide –- only after all these pre-sales have occurred — that you'll be able to move on to presenting the customer with the merchandise they're most likely to want, need, and buy.

Too often, sales professionals jump right to #4, without spending any time working through mandatory sales #1, #2 and #3. Yet it is these primary levels that help you establish the relationship that is so critical to G.R.E.A.T. Selling.

Bear in mind that a customer can buy some of these items within seconds of entering your store. This is particularly true if you work for a retailer with a strong brand. A customer might be pre-sold on the store and experience due to advertising, word of mouth, and/or previous experiences.

However, you should never assume that that is the case. You might work for the most well-known retailer in the world, and still have customers come in who've never heard of your store before! Operate on the assumption that you will have to sell the same four items to each and every customer, and you'll be in a great position!

Additional Thoughts to Consider:

There are two parts to every business transaction: the business part and the human part. The challenge is that some people want a lot, while others don't.

We prefer to do business with people who we like and avoid doing business with people we dislike.

It is easier to sell someone if they like us.

It is easier to take care of problems with a customer if they like us. If they don't like us, the smallest thing becomes an issue.

There are universal turn-offs that block success (not just in selling environments):

When **our self-worth** is struggling and someone makes us feel worthless, we get turned off. That is why in managing people, the management philosophy that works the best is: "The behavior that's rewarded is the behavior that's repeated." Focus on the positive of what someone is doing as opposed to the negative of what someone has done. If someone has done six things right and one thing that is horrible, if you criticize that one thing and don't mention any of the six positives, you will threaten their self-worth.

Road blocks to a goal. There are many examples of people putting road blocks up, but the most universal is when someone tells you, "That won't work." It is frustrating, aggravating, and truly creates irrational behavior.

Expectations not met. I believe this is the root cause of the majority of the problems and challenges we have in business and in our lives today. That is why we can have one of our best customers rave about our store and send in a potential customer, who is turned off. How can this be? It is because the customer who referred the store built it up beyond the expectations of the new customer; therefore, setting the new customer up for disappointment.

Differing values and beliefs (aka, a bad attitude). If we believe our values and beliefs are the right ones and anything else is foolish, unimportant, ridiculous or stupid, that attitude comes through loud and clear.

Bad attitudes are bad for business. They are comprised of three elements:

Facial expressions There are actually 135 facial expressions and there are two groups of people who can read facial expression expertly. They are jury consultants (also experts in body language) and poker players. I recently had a discussion with a professional poker player who said, "The first two hands in a tournament, I look at the people when they first look at their cards. That will set me up for the rest of the game."

Body language What we do with our hands, arms, posture, etc. speaks volumes about our true attitude. In fact, when a person says one thing but their body language says another, trust the body language over the words every time!

Tone of voice I do an exercise in my live programs where I ask the audience to repeat the phrase "good morning" showing different emotions. It really drives home the point that tone of voice affects how our words are received. I will have them say "good morning" happy, sad, tired, disgusted, like they just won the lottery, surprised at a pop quiz, and in a way that tells me to **please stop**. It's amazing how the voices change in unison from emotion to emotion!

Chapter 1 Review

❖ "Service is selling and selling is service."

❖ People do business with people they like

❖ Customer decision-making is *predictably irrational*

❖ The four things you *must* sell
1. Yourself
2. The Store
3. The Experience
4. The Merchandise

❖ Two parts to every business transaction: the business part and the human part

❖ Universal turn-offs that block success

❖ Self-worth is threatened

❖ Road blocks to a goal

❖ Expectations not met

❖ Differing values and beliefs (aka, bad attitudes)

❖ Bad attitudes include:
Facial expressions
Body language
Tone of voice

Chapter 2

THE LIKEABILITY FACTOR

his chapter is about **selling ourselves** by making ourselves as likeable as possible. And the good news is: Anyone can be likeable — if they know how!

Customers don't buy rationally or logically. They buy emotionally.

Logic makes us shop. Logic demands we do price comparisons, shop various offers, and do our homework, then think about it before we make our buying decision. As retailers, logic is not our ally.

Emotions make us buy. Recently a friend of mine went into a store and purchased far more than she ever expected to purchase. All she talked about was how much she loved the salesperson. That behavior is repeated every single day in stores everywhere.

So what's the problem? When was the last time you taught your employees about the steps it takes to be **likeable**? How much business are you losing by **not** teaching your employees to be likeable?

A Parable

"IF I KNEW YOU WERE SO NICE . . ."

I recently bought a new house. I had not met the people I was buying it from until we passed papers. Understand that in any real estate transaction, especially during a down market and challenging times, negotiations get rather heated, to say the least. The reason is that people are selling their home for less than they bought it for, or less than they believe it is worth.

After I met the people, who were the nicest and most delightful people I think I have ever met, I felt bad that I acted like such a jerk during the negotiations. (I actually did all the things I had to do in order to get the house for the price I wanted.) I made a statement without thinking during the closing, which was, "If I knew you were so nice, I probably wouldn't have beaten you up so much on the price." Truth be told, that was a very accurate statement. Of course, you push hard to get the best price, but you pull back a little because of what I refer to as the likeability factor.

Rules of Likeability

There are a number of concrete rules which can be trained and mastered to make yourself (or anyone on your team) more likeable. It is important to understand that there have been many studies showing that attractive people are naturally more likeable. However, there are many beautiful people who simply intimidate and turn people off, as well. I believe that a fat, ugly person who understands the rules of likeability can do very, very well. Trust me, I know, because I have never been accused of looking like Tom Cruise or Brad Pitt, and not too long ago I weighed 90 pounds more than I currently do.

Let's get started. What makes someone likeable?

THE 12 TRAITS OF LIKEABLE PEOPLE

Enthusiastic We love people who are enthusiastic in what they do.

Helpful People who want to pitch in and do more, we tend to like.

Patient We all learn in different ways and at different rates. People who are patient with us are also more likeable.

Happy Being with happy people makes us happy. There is nothing worse than being with someone who suffers from terminal sourpuss-ness!

Interested in Us Toby Keith, the popular country western singer, wrote the song "I Want to Talk About Me." People like people who are interested in them. Good salespeople don't talk about themselves, they talk about the customer.

Flexibility Rigid people are not necessarily the most likeable people. We might respect their position (or not!), but the world is an ever-changing place. People who demonstrate flexibility in their thinking increase their likeability.

The Ability to Ignore Sometimes people will make stupid and hurtful statements. The ability to ignore others' human frailties is a wonderful trait that I wish I could personally master. I had a client I'd been doing business with for 10 years. She made a stupid comment and I criticized her for it. Her reaction was, "Who made you the judge of the universe?" If I had just ignored it, I would have maintained my likeability status — and our relationship.

Communicate in Their Style AARP, the organization for retired people (now for people 50+) publishes a monthly magazine. As their audience has changed to have a young-at-heart attitude, AARP has changed its style. On a recent cover of the AARP magazine there were three featured stories. They were SEX, DRUGS and TONY BENNETT. Now the sex and drugs at 50, 60 or 70 might be different than what their audience might have remembered from their past and the popular phrase "Sex, drugs & rock 'n roll." But Tony Bennett is the same. My point is this: AARP is very clever. They are employing a technique called "mirroring" — essentially communicating in the language of their readers to better connect with their readers.

The Silent Compliment When we ask for someone's opinion and we respect and appreciate it, it goes a long way toward increasing our likeability level.

The Rule of Reciprocity This simply means that if you give something to somebody they will generally like you. Sometimes it is as simple as offering someone a piece of hard candy at a checkout counter. We all know that a free gift with purchase always works.

The Rule of Relevance There is nothing more annoying than dealing with someone who lives in the past. That is not just limited to old people who remember how much better things were "back in the day." It also applies to anyone who loves to talk about their past employer, a past vacation, a past spouse, or a past anything. Be in the moment and be current; it makes you likeable.

The Power of the Compliment If you forget all these other ways of becoming more likeable and just use this one, you will be a winner.

A Parable
EVERYBODY LOVES A COMPLIMENT

I have a collection of Tabasco® ties. The reason I have so many is because I was speaking in New Orleans and I forgot my tie and went to the hotel gift shop to purchase a tie. All they sold were Tabasco® ties, so I bought one. A weird phenomenon occurred. I got a compliment on my tie!

Now that might not seem like a big deal to you, but it was to me, because I am not a HHBL (hunka hunka burning love). I don't get tons of compliments. But I liked getting one! I wore the tie again and again and it almost became my trademark. If you want to know if I liked the tie, the answer is "No!" I think it is one the tackiest ties I have ever owned. And as for Tabasco® sauce, I like my foods bland. Tabasco® sauce to me represents three days in the men's room and a lot of toilet paper. I wear this tie not for myself, but to get compliments. And it never fails!

I was speaking once in Danbury, Connecticut, and was packing up my stuff to leave when the meeting planner enthusiastically said, "Rick, you have to stay, because right after lunch we are hosting a fashion show!" Now, if I never go to another fashion show I will be a happy camper, but I felt obligated, so I stayed. Then in walked the most obnoxious, arrogant man who was so impressed with himself I couldn't stand him. He announced the next exclusive collection from the exclusive collection of such and such designer . . . and named his store. That statement put me into orbit, because I carry the same merchandise in my store! It was not exclusive to him!

The bottom line is this: I didn't like the way he spoke, looked, or the things he had to say. But after his presentation I was a pro and complimented him on his presentation, which finally did work out well. When I introduced myself, he went on and on how thrilled he was to meet me, how much he loved my work, and specifically named one of my books. I was flattered, but when I told him he did a good job, he responded — almost crying — saying, "I will never forget receiving this compliment from you."

Once I realized the guy liked me, I liked him! See how that works?

Chapter 2 Review

✣ We sell ourselves by making ourselves as likeable as possible

✣ Anyone can be likeable — if they know how

✣ Customers don't buy rationally or logically. They buy emotionally.

✣ Logic makes us shop. Emotions make us buy.

✣ The 12 Traits of Likeable People
  Enthusiastic
  Helpful
  Patient
  Happy
  Interested in Us
  Flexibility
  The Ability to Ignore
  Communicate in Their Style
  The Silent Compliment
  The Rule of Reciprocity
  The Rule of Relevance
  The Power of the Compliment

✣ Everyone likes to receive compliments

Chapter 3

DEALING WITH DIFFERENT CUSTOMER PERSONALITIES

As retailers, we deal with many different personality types on a daily basis. Of course each customer is unique, but there is universal agreement that there are four basic personality types. These are the main customer personalities specific to the retail environment.

1. The Director Personality

As the name implies, this personality is generally associated with demanding people. They are the take-charge types. They want what they want when they want it –– and they want it now! In extreme cases they can be intimidating know-it-alls. Directors are generally not into small talk; they want the facts in order to make a decision as quickly as possible.

If you try to get in the way of their goal they will plow through you and, as the expression goes, "take no prisoners." They don't care about anyone's interest other than their own. Their goals are very clear. They want the best possible product at the lowest possible price delivered when they want it — which is usually immediately.

HOW TO DEAL WITH THE DIRECTOR PERSONALITY

Eliminate as much small talk as possible, lay out the facts, give your reasons why they should purchase something and make it brief and to the point. Generally these personality types have high self-esteem, almost to the point of being obnoxious about it.

One of the most valuable tools you can use here is to compliment their direct style and decisiveness. The one thing you never want to do is to tell this personality type they are wrong or they are not listening. You must let them make their own decision. You can try to make suggestions, but make sure they are short and to the point. Remember, the Director gets turned off when you present yourself in any way as a roadblock to their goal.

Remember: Never confront the Director — stay out of their way!

2. The Analytical Personality

These types usually have professions that require accuracy and analysis. These would include jobs such as accountants, engineers or scientists, whereby they conduct research and analyze all the possibilities before making a decision. Just reading that line generally conjures up an image of someone you know who fits the mold, am I right?

MOTIVATORS

What motivates this type of personality when they come into a retail store to buy? Facts, details, product descriptions, *Consumer Reports* information; this personality type wants data. They read manuals, directions and the fine print. Like the Director type they are unaffected by small talk or the niceties that can accompany a retail store visit.

HOW TO DEAL WITH THE ANALYTICAL PERSONALITY

Give them facts and data. Do not make a statement unless you can back it up with pertinent information. If the product has detailed labeling, give it to them. There is one major advantage when it comes to dealing with the analytical personality.

They have done their homework and/or comparative research. In many cases they will actually know more than a salesperson or owner, which makes them a valuable source of information.

Don't be afraid to ask them why they came into your store — because there is a reason. The biggest asset they have is all the research they have done about the product you are selling. And they have it neatly filed away in their iTouch or Smart Phone so it can be easily referenced in seconds.

Analyticals have all of this research and knowledge, yet generally have no one to share it with! Analytical people rarely partner with other analytical people. So they do all this research on a product and their partner could care less about their efforts.

Here is an opportunity for you to be the one who cares! Simply ask them, "What have you learned?" or "Where have you shopped?" They will be thrilled that you asked and will start sharing everything they know. This is where the line "Tell me about..." is so powerful. We can learn a lot about our products and our competition by simply asking the Analytical shopper a few pertinent questions and their opinions.

Remember: Asking someone's opinion is considered the silent compliment.

3. The Belonging (or Relater) Personality

Many times this personality is referred to as the *"Relater."* Relater/Belonging types have a strong need to feel part of a group. I like to use the "my" test on this personality type. This means when a customer refers to "my accountant," "my doctor," "my garage," "my electrician," "my lawyer," or "my store," your store becomes part of their network. These people are usually three calls away from getting anything they want. They always know someone who knows someone who knows someone — the classic example of "three degrees of separation."

HOW TO DEAL WITH THE BELONGING PERSONALITY

The reason we refer to this shopper as the "Belonging Type" is because they take an ownership position in anything they do. The easiest way to sell to this personality type is to simply ask them, "What is your opinion of this product and do you think we should carry it?" Their response might be something like, "I think it looks good and I think you should carry it. I might like something like that. Let me see it." The bottom line is to include them in any way you possibly can, because they want to feel a part of the decision-making process.

One word of caution: The Belonging Type of customer can come into the store when the owner is not there and report back to the owner if someone isn't doing their job. On the plus side, they are wonderful customers to have and a sensational source of never-ending referrals.

Remember: Inclusion is the name of the game with the Belonging customer.

4. The Socializer Personality

Socializers are exactly as the name implies. They are outgoing, love to talk and love to make new friends. The Socializer wants to build a relationship with people who work in the store. This personality type places likeability as one of the most important buying criteria. If they don't like you they are not going to do business with you.

The most important thing to the Socializer is to build friendships. If you talk to them like an Analytical personality, with facts and figures, they will shut right down.

As similar as they might be to the Belonging type, loyalty to one source isn't as important to the Socializer. If they can develop friendships in several different stores then they will go to several different stores.

Socializers love to receive and give compliments. However, they tend to be self-centered. They want to go to a store where they are made to feel important. This is the one group that retailers, owners, managers and salespeople relate to the most, because the majority of retailers will fit in this category!

HOW TO DEAL WITH THE SOCIALIZER PERSONALITY

The most important thing to remember is that it's not all about the merchandise; it is about the relationship. Always remember that the first thing you are selling is **yourself.** You can be giving merchandise away, but the Socializer won't care if they don't like you. Use compliments liberally. Do whatever you have to do to remember the names of these people. Don't lose sight of the fact that although they look at the shopping experience as a fun, social event, your goal is still to sell them merchandise.

Remember: Keep the Socializer focused, yet be light enough to make their shopping experience fun and entertaining.

Dealing with Difficult Personalities

Now let's talk about those difficult customers who ruin our moods, ruin our days, and are a major source of our aggravation. Sometimes we can be in a great mood and have one of these customers from hell and suddenly our great mood is spoiled.

Here we will describe the five most common difficult customer types we retailers are forced to deal with. I get more comments on this one line, not only during seminars, but months and even years afterwards. The line is:

> *Five percent of all customers belong to the PLO: pushy, loud and obnoxious.*

But that's only 5 percent, whereas the rest of our customers are perfectly fine. So the next time a customer is giving you a hard time, think about the fact that they belong to that small, 5 percent PLO group. For any of you who want to know where that 5 percent figure came from, it is based solely on of my 25 years of retail experience. I used to observe that every 20th customer seems a little crazy. It's not scientific. But it's true!

THE FIVE CUSTOMER TYPES FROM HELL AND HOW TO DEAL WITH THEM

1. The Know-It-All Customer

This is the Director type on steroids. They are aloof and arrogant. They will satisfy their need to be a know-it-all by putting salespeople down. Their body language is authoritative. They look down upon you and make themselves feel important by making you feel rotten. Our natural tendency is to prove to them that they are wrong and not put up with their arrogance. We want to put them in their place. Trust me: if you do any of that you will never make the sale.

Don't compete, cope. Don't be afraid to use compliments, as much as it may kill you.

Remember: Never lose sight of the goal to sell merchandise.

2. The Whiner (aka, the Complainer)

These people can see the bad in anything and anyone. If you tell them it is a beautiful sunny day, they reply, "It could rain later." They drive us crazy because everything out of their mouth is negative. They want to pull you down to their level so you can start complaining, too! Our natural tendency would be to say, "Would you shut up already?!"

There's an old story about the waiter who goes up to a table of four whiners and asks, "Is there anything right?" No doubt that waiter didn't get a big tip!

With this type of customer, the best approach is to recognize their point of view but maintain the high road. When they complain about the quality of the merchandise, your store hours or whatever, simply say to them, "I appreciate your point of view and we'll work on that."

> *Remember: Do not try to put them down, lose your temper or go down to their level.*

3. The Picky Customer

As the Know-it-All is the Director on steroids, the Picky type of problem customer is the Analytical gone awry. Picky customers can find the slightest of imperfections, pick up on a word or a phrase a salesperson, manager or owner might say inadvertently and blow it up out of proportion. Just as the Analytical person wants data and facts, the Picky customer looks to find fault with the data and the facts.

There is a difference between the Whiner and the Picky customer. The Picky is not intentionally trying to hurt or insult anyone; they are just constantly aiming for perfection. They are difficult customers because most people just don't think like that. Our natural tendency here is to say, "Give me a break." But if you were to really say that, you would insult the customer and never make a sale.

Remember: It is our job to respect the Picky customer and try to understand and accommodate their behavior. I honestly believe they have no idea.

4. The Wishy-Washy Customer

This is the customer who simply cannot make up their mind. Unfortunately, this category is growing. The first word that will come to your mind is probably *frustrating*. Just when you think they are ready to buy something, they'll change their mind.

They will come in saying they have to have a specific product. You kill yourself to find it and you show it to them. Then they flip-flop and say, "I don't think I really need it." These folks are afraid to make a commitment!

Our natural tendency here is to shake them and say, "Get a life!" However, if you adopt this way of handling the Wishy-Washy customer you will alienate them. The best approach here is to help them to make a decision or make the decision for them. Don't be afraid to use the line "This is what we should do." They will love you; because remember, their fear is about making the decision.

You can counter this by making them feel safe about purchasing from you. Offer Wishy-Washy customers guarantees and a fair return policy within their comfort zone.

Remember: What drives this type of customer is their fear of making a mistake.

5. The Stubborn Customer

This most rigid of customers is an offshoot of the Director. The problem with this type of customer is their lack of flexibility. It's their way or the highway. Again, frustration sets in when you know something is right for them but they rigidly defend the position they have taken and completely lose focus on the bigger picture. Our natural tendency here is to give up or walk away from this type of customer because they're so aggravating. If you do that you will never sell them anything.

That's why the best way to deal with the Stubborn is to always compliment their position and say things such as, "Have you ever considered or thought about an alternative?" In this way you are allowing that customer to save face by making them feel as if the alternative is their idea.

> *Remember: Stubborn customers can be sold — but don't ever try to change their mind! What you do want to do is to offer an alternative or an add-on to their position.*

Internal Customers and External Customers

There are two categories of customers who are often ignored because we fail to realize how important they are. Up to this point we have focused only on the **external customer**. These are the customers who come into our store and buy from us. However, we often ignore our **employees**, or **internal customers,** who in many cases can be some of our very best customers! They are our best customers not only because of the merchandise they purchase from us — even at a discounted price — but because their likes and levels of enthusiasm can influence the sales of many external customers.

Yes they are employees. However, it is our responsibility as owners or managers to create the enthusiasm for our products that will inspire our salespeople to sell them. Don't make the terrible mistake that many retailers make of saying, "They work for me. They should just get out there and sell it." No! You sell it to them first by taking the time to put that product in the most favorable light.

The first sale is to our own salespeople. A great piece of merchandise that isn't loved by the employees isn't a great piece of merchandise. An average piece of merchandise loved by the people who are going to sell it becomes a great piece of merchandise.

> *Remember: The bottom line is to understand the importance of our internal customers who have the ability to make an item hot.*

We need to plan and focus on the process of showing, explaining and yes, even selling our products to our employees. This can be done formally at meetings and informally by managers who understand the features and benefits of the merchandise — and the value of pre-selling it to the store's internal customers.

Chapter 3 Review

❧ Remember that there are two parts of every business transaction — the business part and the human part. The personalities we discussed are:
> The Director who wants control
> The Analytical who seeks facts and data
> The Belonging/Relater who craves the sense of ownership
> The Socializer who is looking for a friend

❧ The sooner we can recognize a customer's personality type, the easier it becomes to sell to them

❧ The customers from hell are basically these personality types on steroids:
> The Know-It-All
> The Whiner
> The Stubborn
> The Picky
> The Wishy-Washy

❧ All need to be better understood if we are to increase sales and make the register ring.

❧ Our greatest source of retail sales is our internal customer, the employee

❧ *What are you doing to address and accommodate all of these customer types?*

Chapter 4

THE G.R.E.A.T. SYSTEM OF SELLING

Okay, now that we've covered some basic nuts and bolts, it's time to delve into what you really need to know to become a GREAT salesperson. G.R.E.A.T. Selling is a process that, once mastered, will transform your performance from O.K. to Wow, or from Wow to Pow, Pow, Powerful!

G.R.E.A.T. Selling Involves Five Distinct Phases

1. Greeting
2. Researching
3. Experimenting and Closing
4. Add-Ons
5. Tethering

Each phase is covered in detail in upcoming chapters.

In case you're in a hurry, here's the ultimate *Cliff Notes* version of *The Retail Sales Bible: The GREAT Book of G.R.E.A.T. Selling*.

Greeting

What to do when the customer comes into the store, how to connect with them and get them talking, and what to do when you've encountered the dreaded, "No thanks, I'm just looking."

Researching

Customers come in carrying a treasure trove of information we can use to help make the sale — but that's never enough. We cover the techniques you need to determine their wants and needs in order to make the sale.

Experimenting and closing

Combine what you've learned about the customer with your knowledge of the store's merchandise to find the absolute perfect items to show the customer. We also discuss presentation and suggest strategies to help you close the sale.

ADD-ONS

One sale is good, but multiple sales are better! Strategies to raise your average customer transaction, each and every time — plus the powerhouse words that will sell more merchandise than you ever thought possible.

TETHERING

Transform a one-buy stand into a long-term relationship by collecting data from your customer and providing the ultimate in follow-up care. Here's how to get the customer to share contact information with you and how to make the most of it!

Chapter 5

GREETING

reeting is the art and science of welcoming the customer to your store. This is the very first thing you should do — and it's the most critical.

Why is greeting so critical?

A lot of things happen. They all take place within the first couple of minutes after a customer enters your store. They immediately do a visual assessment: How does the store look? Is the merchandise appealing? Is the store welcoming?

Does the customer feel like they "belong" in the store?

It is during this brief time period that the customer decides if they are going to buy from you. In a very short time the customer makes some really quick decisions — and many of them are subconscious.

They decide:

If they feel comfortable and at ease in your store

If it seems likely that your store has merchandise they like

If they want to stay or turn around and walk out

Here are the things we can do to influence their decisions to stay and buy. Obviously there are visual merchandising techniques we can employ to positively affect the decision process. But this book is about selling, not visual merchandising.

The GREETING PHASE is comprised of four elements or steps. They are:

1. Your approach to the customer

2. Gathering free information

3. Engaging them in conversation

4. Building a bridge to the next phase

Greeting Phase Step 1: Your Approach to the Customer

From the moment your customer crosses the threshold and enters your store, you have less than one minute to greet them to make them feel welcome.

Some people think that when you first greet the customer you are not selling. Of course you are selling! And as we discussed previously, you are selling yourself first, the store second, the experience third, and the merchandise last. You want to get the customer feeling comfortable in the store. You don't want to pounce on them too soon, because you will only make them feel uncomfortable and seem too pushy.

Greet customers even if you're helping other customers. Every single person who sets foot into your store must be met with a smile and a friendly attitude.

THE WORST OPENING LINES
IN RETAIL SALES

Here is where the first confusion in retail selling occurs. I don't know how it came into being, or why anyone still uses it, but without a doubt, the worst opening line in retail selling is:

"Can I help you?"

I just want to know how it got so popular. It does not work! It is always followed with *"No thanks. I'm just looking."*

The second worst opening lines to use in retail sales greetings are *"How are you today?"* or *"How are you feeling?"*

I pity the poor store clerk who ever asks me how I am feeling, because I am going to tell them. I am going to tell them that I have a pain in my lower back, I have a cut on my leg, my vision is a little cloudy, I am not hearing very well, I have a terrible headache, and my stomach is upset, too. Get the point?

THE #1 MOST EFFECTIVE GREETING IN RETAIL SALES

Over the years, we've tried every greeting known to man. We've also made up a few more. But we keep coming back to one tried-and-true winner. It is so simple and it works every time. And yet I am amazed how few stores use it!

Do you know it? Are you ready to learn it? Here it is, the #1 most effective greeting in retail sales:

"Thanks for coming in!"

Think about it. Your customer has an infinite number of choices and a limited amount of time. They could have done anything. They could have gone to the movies, a museum, a baseball game or Disneyland. They could have decided to stay in and read astronomy textbooks.

But they decided to shop.

Even within that decision, they still have a limitless number of choices. They could have gone online and bought what they wanted without ever leaving their house. They could have gone to a flea market or a garage sale. They could have gone to the big box store down the street. They could have gone to the mall. They could have gone to your competition.

But they chose to come to your store.

Knowing how lucky you are that they decided to shop in your store, is there anything else you could possibly say to them except, "Thanks for coming in"? No, we don't think so, either.

✎ *a random* GREAT *idea* ✎

Never stop greeting! If you pass customers in the store, make sure to acknowledge them with a friendly smile!

FIVE THINGS TO REMEMBER ABOUT GREETING

1. The goal of greeting is to make the customer feel welcome and appreciated.

2. Make eye contact when greeting the customer.

3. Never address a customer from behind — that's scary and creates unwanted pressure.

4. Address customers from a reasonable distance — no shouting across the store.

5. Have a unique, memorable greeting.

Always greet and welcome a customer, even if you're not the one who will be helping them. At this point, the customer is forming an impression of the entire store, so the actions you take now are going to influence their decisions, not only for this visit, but for every subsequent visit they may make to your store.

⟫⟫ *two more random* GREAT *ideas* ⟪⟪

Look the customer in the eye and present a positive attitude!

WHAT COLOR ARE YOUR CUSTOMER'S EYES?

There are some people who believe that to be a GREAT salesperson you must make great eye contact. Frankly, I felt uncomfortable having to look into someone's eyes — until I realized that it is just a quick contact. You are not falling in love, you're just showing interest. If you still feel uncomfortable, focus on the customer's eyebrows or glasses.

Do we really want you to memorize each customer's eye color? No. However, if you focus your salespeople on noticing what color a customer's eyes are, that proves they've at least looked the customer in the eye!

THE POWER OF SMILING

This is one section I get nervous about writing, because I hate dumb, fake smiles, and I don't want anyone to think we are promoting them. However, as we have learned in a previous chapter about the power of likeability, smiling is a major component of being liked and likeable.

It also represents a positive attitude. We want to be with people who are positive, not people who are looking at the negative. When the corners of your mouth are up, you are up, and you bring others up with you!

Greeting Phase Step 2: Gathering Free Information

After your warm, inviting and professional greeting, you want to engage the customer in conversation. This is how we recommend you do it. You want to exchange names for the sake of personalizing the interaction.

This is an example of how this might sound at Uncle Bob's:

"Hi! Thanks for coming in! My name is Bonnie, and you are? Nice to meet you! Is this your first time in our store?"

This welcome accomplishes a number of things:

It welcomes the customer and puts them at ease.

It expresses gratitude for their presence.

It is also a form of compliment, because you are compliment-ing the decision they have made in coming into the store.

It provides the sales associate's name.

It collects the customer's name, which can be used again throughout the sales process. This strengthens the rela-tionship. There is nothing sweeter to the ears than hear-ing one's own name.

But, the key aspect of the above exchange is asking the cus-tomer if they have been in the store before. That's **free information**, and there's more where that came from.

GATHERING FREE INFORMATION

Conventional wisdom says there's no such thing as a free lunch, and do you know what? Conventional wisdom is right. Free lunches are few and far between!

However, during this step of the greeting, your cus-tomer is providing all kinds of free information you can use during the upcoming conversation. You can use this free in-formation to help you customize and personalize the offer-ings you make during the EXPERIMENTING PHASE (discussed in a later chapter).

Savvy sales professionals must be observant of the silent cues a customer provides.

EXAMPLES OF SILENT CUES

Clothing preference/style (sports logos, band names, or brand symbols)

Jewelry, tattoos, or other personal decoration

The type of car, truck, motorcycle or other vehicle the customer arrived in

Items carried (purse, briefcase, diaper bag, bags from other stores)

Literature carried (sales flyers, pages from magazines, *Consumer Reports*)

People they're shopping with (spouse, parent, small children, teen children, friends)

Body language: do they seem nervous, in a hurry, irritated, tired, excited or cheerful?

You can use much of this information as a starting point for subsequent conversation, or use the data gathered here to help you make more appropriate suggestions during the EXPERIMENTING PHASE of the sale.

Be observant without being judgmental. You cannot determine how much money someone has, what their credit rating is, how likely they are to buy, or what their station in life is based solely on physical appearance — or even all of these silent cues combined!

RICK SAYS

In fact, the more money someone has, the less likely they are to look like they have any money! It's called "stealth wealth." Rich people don't want to look rich.

Read The Millionaire Next Door *and you'll discover that the people with the most wealth drive secondhand cars and wear the same kind of clothes you and I do!*

⟞ *another random* **GREAT** *idea* ⟝

If the customer does not offer their name
when you tell them yours, ask them!!

Here's an example of this in action at Uncle Bob's General Store:

Bonnie: Hi! Thanks for coming in! Welcome to Uncle Bob's! My name is Bonnie. And you are?

Customer: Hi, I'm Max.

Bonnie: Nice to meet you, Max! Is this your first time in our store?

This might seem a little formal, especially if you're trying it for the first time. Remember you're trying to set the tone for the entire shopping experience, one in which you want the customer to like and trust you.

You'll see that this greeting accomplishes the five functions outlined earlier. Most important of all, it leads us into Step 3: Engaging the Customer in Conversation.

➤ *yet another random* GREAT *idea* ➤

Practice gathering free information.

You can do this anywhere — at the grocery store, at the mall, on the beach, out dancing with your friends. Work with a partner, and discover how much you can learn about a person without ever saying a word. Compare notes. Who picked up more cues? What did your partner notice that you didn't? What did you pick up on that they missed? Being observant is a skill you can teach yourself!

Greeting Phase Step 3: Engaging Them in Conversation

Engaging the customer in conversation is just a fancy way of saying "Get them talking!" Why is it important to get the customer talking? It's simple: The more the customer talks to you, the more likely he or she will be to like and trust you. People buy from people they like and trust.

Very few customers will spontaneously start conversations with you all on their own. You have to give them a little boost to get the words going — a phrase or question that will launch the conversation.

If you look back at the two examples we gave for the customer approach (Step 1), you might notice something. Both examples end with the question **"Is this your first time in our store?"**

There's a reason for this!

Asking this question opens up a whole realm of conversational possibilities for you. The customer is going to give you one of two answers. They're either going to say "yes" or they're going to say "no."

DEALING WITH THE REPEAT VISITOR/CUSTOMER

If the customer says "no" you're in a great position. This isn't their first time in the store, which means they've been in your store before, they liked what they experienced, and they've decided to come back. These customers have already, on some level, made the decision to buy.

When you're attempting to engage the customer who has been in your store before, you have a few options. You can say:

"Great! It's fantastic to have you back again! What did you purchase the last time you shopped with us?"

OR

"Welcome back! How is your last purchase working out for you?"

These questions have something in common: They're structured in such a way that customers have to say more than "yes" or "no" to answer you. Open-ended questions like these are very effective at getting the conversation going. In fact, the second response, in particular, is very effective because it allows to you to find out what they liked or didn't like about their last purchase. This will tell you volumes about what they might be looking for — or want to avoid!

➤ *and another random* GREAT *idea* ➤

To get the customer talking, ask open-ended questions.

An open-ended question is a question that cannot be answered with a simple "yes" or "no" response. To answer the question, the customer has to give you more information!

The following are examples of open-ended questions:

How's your last purchase working out for you?

When will you be wearing these shoes?

What did you use the last time you had this problem?

What did you like most about your last _____?

How often do you typically need to use _____?

See? None of these questions can be answered with a simple "yes" or "no." When the customer answers you, you'll achieve two things:

1. You'll learn valuable information you can use later during the EXPERIMENTING PHASE.

2. You'll have started the conversation — and the sales process!

Dealing with the First-time Visitor/Customer

Customers who answer "yes" are letting you know this is their first time in the store.

That's when you know you're standing at the make-or-break moment. Everything will hinge on this moment. You have the golden opportunity to set the tone for the remainder of the customer's shopping experience with your reply.

QUICK REVIEW: THE FOUR ITEMS EVERY CUSTOMER HAS TO BUY

Before we reveal your reply options when you're attempting to engage the first-time customer in conversation, let's stop and review the four items every customer **has** to buy (from Chapter 2). The customer has to buy into these concepts long before they'll consider purchasing anything:

1. YOURSELF

2. THE STORE

3. THE EXPERIENCE

4. THE MERCHANDISE

Understanding these four items will help you comprehend what you're trying to do now, during this initial conversation with the customer.

Each opportunity is a critical point. If the customer doesn't like what they encounter at any given stage along the way, chances are they're not going to buy from you. Even if they do buy something — and there will always be those customers who make an "obligatory" purchase because they hate to go into a store without buying something — they won't be coming back. You won't have converted them from simply "a" customer into "your" customer.

When a customer says they've never shopped with you before, it's an open invitation to brag a little about your store and to share your company's philosophies.

Why would you want to do that?

People like to buy from the best — and your customers are no different! Letting them know the good things about your store instills a certain amount of confidence in them. They'll feel more comfortable about the store and buying from you.

Also, you're making them feel comfortable that you will be around to help them after the purchase.

Service is incredibly important, particularly if you're selling expensive merchandise such as computers, lawn tractors, fine jewelry — in short, any purchase that might need some follow-up attention down the road.

A good deal is always attractive, but for some customers, knowing that there's someone standing behind that good deal, someone who will be there over the long haul, is even more important!

WHAT SHOULD YOU BRAG ABOUT?

At Uncle Bob's General Store, Bonnie, Bill and Beth have been trained to let customers know their store offers the widest selection for 100 miles, and that everything is guaranteed for life, period. No questions asked, ever.

Every store will have its own set of facts to brag about — from the range of merchandise to price deals to guarantees to the superbly talented personnel. In marketing textbooks, they call these facts **unique selling propositions**, which is a fancy way to say:

"This is what makes our store cool!"

We'll be using the phrase *pride points* throughout this book to refer to unique selling propositions. It's easier than writing out "the things that make your store cool" 500 times.

Telling customers about your **pride points** shares with them what makes your store special. And special is why the customer is shopping in your store instead of the competition's store!

Think about it: You're a specialty store or department. Special's right there in the name!

Your store may already have an established set of pride points they want the sales team to use. If not, you can generate your own list. Possible pride points to consider include:

Merchandise selection

Exclusivity: We are the only store that carries Brand X

Expert knowledge and assistance

Education

A fun shopping experience

An atmosphere that makes customers feel at home and welcome

Low prices

Guarantees on your merchandise, prices or service

Customer service

Generous return policies

Sales event or promotion

The store's personality

Local or family ownership

Here are a few examples of how this conversation works at Uncle Bob's:

Beth: Is this your first time in our store?

Customer: Yeah, first time.

Beth: Well, we're glad to have you. Hey, did you know we offer the largest selection of sporting equipment and furniture for 100 miles? Uncle Bob has a comparison shopping program to make sure we've got the best prices, too. If you can find a lower price advertised anywhere, we'll match it — and pay you $100!

Customer: Wow!

Beth: Plus, we do custom orders. So if you don't find what you're looking for today, we'll work with you to make sure you feel comfortable with any decision you make. So, what part of your lifestyle are we working on today?

Another example:

Bill: Is this your first time in our store?

Customer: Yeah. My friend came in a couple of weeks ago, and she told me I have to check this place out. So I decided to stop in and see what all the hoopla is about.

Bill: Great! Let me tell you a little bit about us. We believe in giving the customer the ultimate power: the power of choice! That's why we have the largest selection of merchandise for 100 miles! We have a low price guarantee and with our non-commissioned staff, you can feel confident that you are making the right choice, not the highest-price choice!

Customer: That's interesting. You guys aren't on commission?

Bill: Nope. Our commitment to you is to help you make the best decision possible. So what part of your lifestyle are we working on today?

MAKING THIS TECHNIQUE YOUR OWN

Now, every store is different. We can't all work for Uncle Bob! So you might have to tweak this a little bit to make it work for you. The idea is to point out those things your store is proud of and that differentiate you from the competition. Use pride points to illustrate what makes your store special. This will make your customers feel good about shopping with you.

There might be a few things that differentiate your store from other stores in the area. You don't want to list each and every thing. You want to focus on the **exciting difference**: the one that makes your store fun, the one that will get customers talking about you!

The customer has to feel good about shopping with you. More than that, they have to be excited about the experience. On some level, they've got to know they're going to have fun.

THE ABSOLUTE MASTER OF FUN
AND EXCITEMENT: DISNEY

Disney tells their employees (who they refer to as "cast members") that **everything sells**. When a customer looks at a trashcan in Disneyland, they know they're in Disneyland because the trashcan talks, or it's been pressed into service as a musical instrument. The smallest detail is important to Disney, because they know their customers are **there to have fun**.

Customers come to your store to have fun, too! They're probably not expecting quite as much fun as they'd have at Disneyland, but they're still looking for a good time.

That's critical. Just because someone walks in your doors and is looking around at your merchandise doesn't mean they want to buy from you. It means they're looking for a good time shopping.

Getting them in the door is the first step. As we discussed in the Four Levels of Selling, you still have some selling to do!

Now it's show time. You have to convince your customer that your store is the best place in the world to shop!

Where you buy something is just as important as what you buy. This is true for many, many shoppers. You might even feel this is true for yourself. Think about it:

What do you buy from a *specific* store, just because it is *that* store?

⤜ *a random* GREAT *idea* ⤛

Never underestimate the power of a bright smile
and eye contact when greeting any customer.
It shows you are sincere and genuine.

⤜ *another random* GREAT *idea* ⤛

Use the free information to encourage the customer to talk.

Remember all that **free information** we talked about? All
that insider information we could learn about our customers
in the first three to four minutes of their time in our store?
Free information includes all those clues and cues the customer gives us as a signal about who they are and what they
value. These "silent cues" include:

Clothing preference/style (sports logos, band names, or
   brand symbols)

Jewelry, tattoos, or other personal decoration

The type of car, truck, motorcycle or other vehicle the
   customer arrived in

Items carried (purse, briefcase, diaper bag, bags from
   other stores)

Literature carried (sales flyers, pages from magazines,
   Consumer Reports)

People they're shopping with (spouse, parent, small children, teen children, friends)

Body language: do they seem nervous, in a hurry, irritated, tired, excited or cheerful?

Use this free information to get the customer talking! A simple "What a great necklace!" has sold more dresses than you could ever imagine!

Greeting Phase Step 4: Building the Bridge to the Next Phase

So now you have used the pride points and you have gathered your free information and you have engaged the customer in conversation. There should be absolutely no problem selling to this customer, right? Once you get through this fabulous introduction, all you have to do is ring up the order, right?

If it was that easy, there wouldn't be much need for a Retail Sales Bible, would there?

Sadly (although admittedly, luckily for us!), it's not quite as easy as that. Once you've greeted the customer and engaged them in conversation, you're ready to move onto the next step toward the sale ... but we're not quite at the closing stage yet.

BUILDING A BRIDGE

What is a bridge? A bridge is the part of the conversation you use to build a connection with your customer. It's a chance to communicate. While you're gathering information from the customer, the customer is learning to trust you!

The bridge builds a connection between you and your customer. It's how you transition from "Thanks for coming in!" to the actual selling. More importantly, this is your chance to determine if the customer really is "just looking" (it does happen, especially if your store is located within a mall), or if they really want to buy and just need a little reassurance.

There are two parts of an effective bridge: **Soften** and **Ask**.

Part One: Soften When a customer says they're "just looking," GREAT salespeople offer a response that lets the customer know they understand their desire to look around. After all, haven't you ever gone into a store simply because you wanted to see what was in there?

Here are some lines to use in this situation:

"I understand how you feel. When you are trying to make a good decision, it's important to take your time."

"No problem! I can certainly appreciate wanting to take your time and look around; after all, we have the largest selection in town!"

"Absolutely! We've got a ton of new merchandise in this month. You're going to have a great time checking it all out!"

The key to **softening** the "just looking" response is to let the customer know it is okay to be just looking. Express your understanding of their situation. After all, you have been in their shoes and you do know how they feel!

Part Two: Ask Once you've softened the customer, then you **ask**. Ask what? Ask a question! Why ask a question now? For three reasons:

1. You're continuing to engage the customer in conversation.

2. This is your chance to determine if the customer truly is "just looking" or if they have a specific want or need in mind that you could assist them with.

3. Finally, and perhaps most important, it lets the customer know that you want to help them. When they're ready to transition from casual browsing to serious shopping, they know you'll be there for them.

This is one of the keys to likeability. Being available to the customer and demonstrating a genuine and sincere desire to help them is G.R.E.A.T. Selling.

 Here are some Great Ask Questions: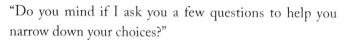

"Do you mind if I ask you a few questions to help you narrow down your choices?"

"If you wouldn't mind, I'd like to ask you a couple of quick questions to point you in the right direction and save you some time."

"Would you like me to show you the hot sellers? I can highlight some of our best merchandise and save you some time."

HOW THE ASK QUESTIONS WORK

Ask Questions have two components:

1. You're asking for permission to ask further questions.

2. You're pointing out the benefit of the answers — usually to save the customer time.

Everyone wants to save time!

Here's how it works at Uncle Bob's General Store:

Customer: I'm just looking.

Bonnie: That's great! I can understand why you'd want to take your time and look around — Uncle Bob's has the widest selection for 100 miles. We certainly have a lot to choose from! But if you wouldn't mind, I'd like to ask you a few questions to help you narrow down some of the choices and maybe save you some time today. Would that be okay?

OR

Customer: That's great to know, but really I'm just looking today . . .

Bill: Hey, I completely understand! The holidays are coming up, and you want to make a wise decision when picking out gifts. But I know you've got a really busy schedule, so if it would be okay, I'd love to ask you a few questions to help you narrow down your choices.

OR

Customer: Thanks, but I really am just looking!

Beth: Great! I will check back with you in a few minutes!

This lets the customer know you won't leave them out on a limb. You're accountable now to return to assist them. Meanwhile, they've got the luxury to look around to their heart's content.

You can also try a little humor. Saying, "That's fine, just don't look over there!" can create curiosity and get your customer laughing. Another variation on this idea is to say, "You can look — but no touching!"

The bridge works! But you have to know the secret. Would you like to know the secret?

Here it is: ***The Bridge only works if you use it!***

We have so many stories — hundreds and hundreds and hundreds of stories — of customers saying "I'm just looking." The salesperson gives up, letting the customer go. The customer is literally headed to the door, on their way to the parking lot, when the store manager sees them, uses a bridge, and before you know it, sells them something!

Building the bridge accomplishes several things:

You're helping the customer get ready to shop.

You're lowering the walls of sales resistance.

You're eliminating some of the customer's fears and hesitations.

ELIMINATING CUSTOMER FEAR AND HESITATION

It might seem strange to think about your customer having fears and hesitations. After all, you're working in a specialty shop, not a house of horrors!

However, some customers have a lot of anxiety about shopping. They may have had previous experiences that created fears and hesitations within them. They don't want to repeat the mistakes or negative experiences they've been through before.

Picture those fears and anxieties as a deep, dark pit in the Earth. If you've ever stood on the edge of a canyon or crevasse and looked down, you know that stomach-churning, nerve-rattling feeling of fear.

When you're at the edge of a canyon, the fear is of falling to your death.

When you're at the threshold of a store, the fear is of making a mistake, spending your money foolishly, or being pressured into purchasing things you really don't want.

Fear can be overwhelming. After all, you don't want to risk jumping over the scary, dark canyon — you might fall in and perish!

But if there was a clear, safe way to get from one side of the canyon to the other, jumping wouldn't be so scary, would it? In fact, if there was a strong, secure bridge, built of metal and ready to withstand all kinds of pressure and weather, you might not even think about the canyon yawning wide beneath your feet!

In selling, your goal is to build a relationship with your customer and make them like and trust you. The flip side of this is taking away their fear: their fear of making a mistake, their fear of being sold something they didn't want.

How do you remove fear? Increase your likeability, share your pride points, and build that bridge that moves your customers from looking to buying!

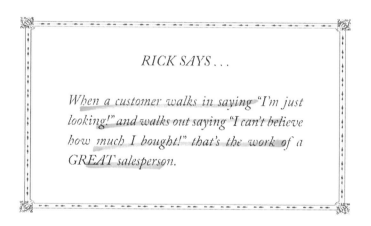

RICK SAYS . . .

When a customer walks in saying "I'm just looking!" and walks out saying "I can't believe how much I bought!" that's the work of a GREAT salesperson.

Chapter 5 Review

→ Greeting is the art and science of welcoming the customer to your store. The greeting is comprised of:

> Your approach to the customer
> Gathering free information
> Engaging them in conversation
> Building a bridge to the next phase

→ The worst opening lines in retail sales:
> *"Can I help you?"*
> *"How are you today?"*
> *"How are you feeling?"*

→ The #1 most effective greeting in retail sales
> *"Thanks for coming in!"*

→ Five Things to Remember About Greeting

1. The goal of greeting is to make the customer feel welcome and appreciated.

2. Make eye contact when greeting the customer.

3. Never address a customer from behind — that's scary and creates unwanted pressure.

4. Address customers from a reasonable distance — no shouting across the store.

5. Have a unique, memorable greeting.

- ✦ Engage the customer in conversation

- ✦ Gather free information

- ✦ Silent cues

- ✦ Be observant without being judgmental

- ✦ Dealing with the repeat visitor/customer

- ✦ Dealing with the first-time visitor/customer

- ✦ Pride points = what makes your store cool

- ✦ Customers come to your store to have fun

- ✦ The bridge builds a connection between you
  and your customer

- ✦ There are two parts of an effective bridge:
    Soften
    Ask

- ✦ The Bridge only works if you use it

- ✦ Eliminate customer fear and hesitation

- ✦ When a customer walks in saying, "I'm just
  looking!" and walks out saying, "I can't believe
  how much I bought!" that's the work of a
  GREAT salesperson!

Chapter 6

RESEARCHING

What comes to mind when you hear the word "research"? Do you picture a scientist in a lab, peering intently into test tubes? Maybe you think of a detective, out in the field, trying to gather evidence? Or you envision a doctor, tracking down mysterious symptoms in an effort to cure a patient?

All of these examples have something in common: they involve a skilled professional paying attention and asking questions, listening carefully to the answers, and probing further.

That's exactly what a GREAT salesperson needs to do!

After completing all the steps of GREETING the customer, we move into the RESEARCHING PHASE. You will want to learn as much as you can about the customer, for several reasons.

You see, the more we know about the customer, the easier it becomes to:

Bond with the customer

Make appropriate suggestions

Sell to the customer

The Three A's

One of the goals we have during the RESEARCHING PHASE is to learn each customer's Three A's. The Three A's are the essential qualities any suggestion to the customer must have.

There are no guarantees in sales. Nothing is 100%! However, if all of your suggestions incorporate the Three A's, you've got a far greater chance of making the sale.

When a suggestion incorporates the Three A's, it is:

1. *Accurate.* Merchandise that will fulfill the customer's stated wants or needs.

2. *Appropriate.* Merchandise that is the best option to fulfill the customer's wants or needs — not necessarily the most expensive or popular, but the best.

3. *Appealing.* Merchandise that will make the customer say, "Oh yes!" or "Wow!" or "That's it!" Something they cannot resist — nor would they want to!

PLAYING DOCTOR

One of the best ways to think about research is to think about the experience you have when you go to the doctor.

Generally, most people don't go to the doctor "just because." They have a reason to go to the doctor, even if they're not sure exactly what the outcome will be.

They may not feel well. They may be tired. They may have grown an extra toe. Whatever the case may be, they have a reason to visit the physician.

THE SAME IS TRUE FOR SPECIALTY STORES

If you're a specialty retailer, you can rest assured that the vast majority of customers who come into your store are there for a reason.

For example, if you sell men's suits, it's a safe bet that most of the customers in the store have at least some interest in men's suits.

If a customer has never, ever worn anything except greasy jeans and ripped t-shirts — even on his wedding day — and he has absolutely no plans on changing his attire, guess what? He's not coming to your store!

People who don't fish will seldom set foot in a bait and tackle shop. Women who don't do crafts typically don't frequent craft supply stores. People who live in high-rise apartments have little reason to visit lawn and garden shops.

There are always exceptions, of course. You'll get people who are looking for gifts for people who do usually shop in that type of store, even if they, themselves, do not. A son-in-law might be an avid fisherman. A mother might need to buy supplies for her daughter's school service project. High-rise apartment dwellers might have parents who are gardening fanatics.

However, these customers are generally easy to deal with. They know they need help and generally aren't shy about asking for it!

The vast majority of people who come to a specialty store, however, know why they are there. They might not know *exactly* why they are there, but they have a vague or even a pretty good idea. They have a need or a want, and they know your store is the type of store that can help them meet that need or want.

❧ *a random* GREAT *idea* ❧

Ask the right questions so you can figure out
what the customer is looking for.

Remember, if you've reached the RESEARCHING PHASE with a customer, you're in the driver's seat. The customer **will buy from you** — if you do a good job from this point forward.

But let's go back to the doctor's office for a moment. You're not feeling well and you're not sure what's wrong, exactly. What does the doctor do? How does she determine what is wrong? She asks questions! She listens to the answers!

A doctor needs more than a vague "I don't feel right" to help you feel better. The doctor asks questions to collect the information she needs to make an informed diagnosis.

Doctors have to choose their questions carefully. They do this because they need to determine exactly what may be causing the problem and rule out things that aren't the cause. They can't guess, because if they guess wrong, someone could die.

Now, no one's going to die if you recommend the wrong merchandise. However, the importance of asking the right questions to make the right "diagnosis" is the same. When a customer comes to the store, you must take the time to figure out what the customer is looking for.

You do this by asking questions.

This sounds so simple — **yet 99.9 percent of salespeople never do this**. Customers are left to flounder around on their own, or are asked a question or two and then presented with the merchandise the sales professional *thinks* they want to buy.

By researching the customer's wants and needs, you'll be providing an experience that is completely different from what they've experienced at other stores and with other salespeople. Playing doctor this way actually gives you a **competitive advantage**!

EARNING THE CUSTOMER'S TRUST

What happens when you fail to take the proper time to re-search the customer? Let's be realistic: it's easier and faster to skip this step and jump right to ADD-ONS. But what happens if you take the easy, fast way out?

Customer dissatisfaction

Wasted time and effort

High returns

Lost opportunity for multiple sales

Lower average sales

No sales at all

Customer doesn't come back to the store

Customer loses confidence in you

Customer loses confidence in your store

RESEARCH IS WORTH THE TIME AND EFFORT

You'll sell more units of merchandise and you'll sell more in dollar amount. The more you know about the customer, the more options you'll be able to extend to them. You can even introduce categories of merchandise they may not have thought about or planned to purchase that day. On the other end of the sale, proper research cuts down on returned merchandise.

WHAT ARE YOU DOING WHEN YOU'RE RESEARCHING?

You're making a customer comfortable and open to buying from you by gaining their trust. How does that work? Like this:

When the customer trusts you, when they feel like you've done a good job taking care of them, they're going to come back and see you again.

It is far, far easier to sell to a repeat customer than it is to a brand new customer who has never been in the store before. That's the value of the relationship: establishing the fact that the customer can trust and depend upon you will help your sales today and in the future!

CONDUCTING EFFECTIVE RESEARCH

Conducting research in the retail environment requires asking questions. The questions you ask are very important and they will vary with what type of store you work in.

The purpose behind the questions remains constant. You ask questions to help customers identify and articulate their needs and wants. This process gets to the heart of what they are looking for!

Think like a doctor. Ask questions like a doctor. You want to discover:

The need or problem

The symptoms of the need or problem

When and where and why the problem or need is occurring

Understanding Wants vs. Needs

During the RESEARCHING PHASE, we're working on discovering the customer's wants and needs. This whole process gets a lot easier if we understand what "wants" are, what "needs" are, and what the relationship between the two is.

WHAT ARE NEEDS?

If we were going to look in the dictionary, we'd discover that a **need** is an item essential for survival. If you don't have what you need, you're not going to make it.

Basic needs include food, water, shelter, and protection from the elements.

People buy what they need because they need it. It's very basic. You might feel guilty buying something just because you **want** it — but if it's something you **need**, it's a lot easier to open up your wallet.

Look around your store.

Chances are that what you're looking at are not needs. No one ever died for the lack of a pearl necklace or a flat-screen television.

You don't find needs for sale in a specialty store. What you find are wants. But that's okay, because a GREAT salesperson can transform wants into needs.

WHAT ARE WANTS?

Wants are everything else. **If it's not a need, it's a want.** We want lots of things. We want great clothes and awesome electronics, new books and fantastic gifts for our friends, shiny jewelry on our fingers and stylish shoes on our toes.

The Rolling Stones were wrong, in case you were wondering. Today's customer has learned that you often *can* get what you want!

That being said, most customers are far more comfortable purchasing needs than wants.

That means you, as a GREAT salesperson, have to learn a little bit of magic. You need to be able to *convert a want into a need.*

The GREAT salesperson has a mission during the RE-SEARCHING PHASE: to discover the customer's want and help the customer convert it into a need. This makes it easier for the customer to buy! Why? Because we're more comfortable buying what we need than justifying buying what we simply want.

A Parable
TRANSFORMATION

Recently, I lost quite a bit of weight and my clothes weren't fitting right anymore. They fit, mind you — just not right.

A GREAT salesperson will use research to discover that while I don't necessarily **need** any new pants (I have a closet full of clothes), I **want** new pants to show off how thin I am now!

Then, using all the tools at his or her disposal, that GREAT salesperson will talk to me about all the benefits new pants will provide and point out how good and thin and fantastic I'll feel when I'm wearing them. In the process, this GREAT salesperson will transform my **want** into a **need.**

And guess what? I will buy new pants!

Listening and Likeability

Customers buy from salespeople they like. How do you make customers like you? You listen to them!

The rarest thing in the world is a good listener! We're all so busy talking, talking, talking all the time that very few of us actually pause to take in what anyone else is saying.

This results in a lot of noise, but not a whole lot of communication!

Practice listening to your customers. Focus on what they're saying to you. They're giving you all the information you need to make a great sale!

HOW TO LISTEN

Listening is a learned skill. Don't feel bad if you're not a great listener right now. It's something you can pick up quickly, especially if you practice these tips:

Face your customer Look at your customer! Make eye contact! It's hard for customers to take you seriously or trust you if you're looking at other customers, the stock on the shelves, the ceiling, your co-workers, etc.

Focus on the customer's words Listen while your customer is speaking. **Do not** use this time to think up what you're going to say back to them. Too often, we're so focused on crafting a great reply, we reply to something totally different than what the customer actually said!

Don't interrupt It's so easy to hear part of the customer's description of their needs and say, "Wait! I have just the thing!" Then we scamper off to the shelves to retrieve the merchandise. However, doing this too soon cuts off the entire conversation. You need to hear the customer out to get a complete picture of their wants and needs!

Encourage further conversation Little statements of agreement, such as "I see," "Yes, I know the feeling," or "I hear what you're saying," indicate that you're paying attention and want to hear more from the customer.

Mirror the customer's words Repeat back to the customer what they said to you. This doesn't have to be verbatim — a brief summary will work wonders. If you want to remember a particular point to use later (and you probably will), don't be afraid to mirror it back to the customer as soon as you hear them say it!

A Parable
THE FRAME GAME

My mother was an artist. One of my prized possessions is a set of four ceramic plates that she painted. They're just beautiful! I would like you to see them!

When my wife and I redecorated our house, we decided to have the plates framed in shadow boxes so we could display them properly. We wrapped up the plates and went down to the local chain arts & crafts store.

We had a lot of questions about the job. I wanted to make sure that the plates would look good and that they'd be secure; after all, if they fell out of the frame and shattered, they could not be replaced! These plates are truly treasures to me.

I was talking to the young man working in the framing department about the plates when the manager walked by. He took one look at the plates, still nestled in the newspaper we'd wrapped them in, and sneered. "You do realize it's going to be at least $25 apiece to frame those?"

I was taken aback. "I wasn't asking about the price, I was asking if you had the capabilities to do the job."

Apparently this guy didn't like my tone any more than I liked his. Before you could count to three, he had hustled us out of the store.

My wife and I decided to stop at a little frame shop on the corner, a specialty shop that we'd never been in before.

From the start, it was a completely different experience. The salesman's eyes went wide when he saw the plates. He complimented what a fantastic job my mother had done painting them. Then he listened to my concerns about keeping the plates securely mounted in the frames.

Then I said, "I was thinking maybe we'd use black velvet for the background."

"Oh no!" he said. "The risk of oxidization is too high. You wouldn't want that."

I don't know the first thing about oxidization, but I sure agreed with that salesman: it sounded bad, and I didn't want it! I listened to his suggestions about how to frame the plates, agreeing to what he said. It was clear that he was very knowledgeable about framing.

Finally, we had the plates laid out, in a demonstration of what they'd look like, in the frame he'd suggested.

That's when he paused, looking down at the plates. He looked down at the plates for quite a while. So long, in fact, that I was beginning to worry that there was something wrong with him!

I asked, "Sir, are you all right?"

He looked up with a smile. "I was just thinking," he said, "how proud your mother would be right now."

That cinched the sale! When we walked out, we'd spent a little over $400 to have mother's plates framed — and it was worth every penny!

Had the manager in the first store **listened,** he would have **heard** that price was not our most important concern. *Never assume that price is what's driving your customer.* Listen to what your customer is saying! They will reveal what **is** driving them and you can tailor your response accordingly.

The Three Factors that Influence Your Customers

Your customer's thoughts, wants, needs, and desires regarding your merchandise are influenced in three ways. They are:

1. Past experience with the product

2. New expectations of the product

3. Conditions of use for the new product

These three factors can serve as a starting point when you're crafting a list of questions to ask the customer. Remember, no two customers are the same. Each one comes to you with a unique set of experiences, expectations, and attitudes. That means you can't have a one-size-fits-all set of questions that will suit every circumstance.

However, if you start with a prepared list of questions, you can adapt and customize your questions from this starting point.

There are literally hundreds of questions you could ask a customer — if you had the time and they were willing to stand in your store talking all day! That's not too likely. The key is to find the right balance.

PAST EXPERIENCE

You want to ask the most essential questions first. One of the easiest ways to do this is by starting with past experiences. Asking what the customer has now generates information you can use when extending options later.

For example, you might ask one of the following:

Tell me about the shoes you're wearing now.

What did you wear to the last big event you attended?

How did you handle the slugs in your yard last year?

What have you tried to solve your cat's hairball problem?

In some cases, you'll discover that the customer loves what they have right now and they want to purchase more like it. That's easy enough, right? In other cases, you'll learn that the customer has had a bad experience and they want anything but the product they used previously.

Here are some great questions for determining past experience:

Tell me about the _____ you're using now.

What do you like best about the _____ you're using now?

What do you like least about the _____ you're using now?

What would you change or do differently this time?

What is your favorite _____? Why?

How often do you shop for a new _____?

What style/model of _____ have you found works best for you?

NEW EXPECTATIONS

Another starting point you can use is customer expectations. Asking a customer about their expectations will help you identify what they think is important and what features they want their new purchase to have. This makes it easier to narrow down your selection. If a customer wants a camera they can carry around on their biking and hiking trips, you can immediately eliminate all large, cumbersome, heavy cameras from your options list.

Expectations are a very important component of research.

Understanding your customer's expectations:

Cuts down on returns

Eliminates disappointment with the purchase

Minimizes buyer's remorse

Helps build trust

Here are some GREAT questions to determine customer expectations:

What would be the most important thing to consider in your new _____?

What have you heard about, read about, or had a friend recommend _____?

What brands of _____ are you familiar with? Which ones do you prefer?

How do you expect your new _____ to help you (at work, at home, while you're traveling, etc.)?

Have you used a _____ before?

How do you plan to use your new _____?

What's more important to you, price or _____? (For this one, fill in the blank with the most appropriate choice: comfort, style, durability, performance, size, etc.)

REASONABLE EXPECTATIONS

Customers can have realistic, reasonable expectations of what a new product can do for them. Or they might have expectations that aren't realistic.

For example, a customer might rationalize that if a $50 pair of running shoes lasts six months, then a $100 pair should last a year. While that might make mathematical sense, it doesn't translate to reality. Price isn't the determining factor in how long a pair of shoes will last, mileage and usage conditions are.

Discovering your customer's expectations — especially the unrealistic ones — is a big help. This is your opportunity to present some education to help the customer make an informed decision. This is crucial in helping the customer avoid disappointment!

If we're going to look at the running shoe example, a GREAT salesperson might say something like:

"It sounds to me like you're concerned about buying a pair of running shoes that will last a long time. Let me show you some of our most durable shoes that can stand up to the most rugged running conditions."

Notice we didn't mention price here. Price isn't the customer's primary concern: it's getting value for the money. A shoe that will last a long time will deliver more value to this customer. Greater durability will make the customer happy with their purchase.

WHAT ABOUT PRICE?

Price isn't always the issue — but there are times when it is the primary issue. Some customers are price-driven. That number on the price tag is more important than any feature or benefit you could show them. Other customers don't care about price. They want what they want, and they'll pay whatever it takes to get that. Most customers fall somewhere between these two extremes.

Nine times out of ten, a customer will not bring up price!

It's up to you to start that conversation. Here's how you can be proactive and successfully address the issue of price with your customers.

Remember that your store has a large selection of products. Chances are there's a wide range of prices, which allows customers to feel confident they can afford buying from your store.

Your job is to help the customer make the best decision possible, so they can strike a balance between selecting the product that best meets their want (which you deftly convert to a need) and the amount of money they are willing to spend.

You should work the expectation question about price into the process with every customer. Never assume that you can tell how much a customer wants to spend based upon their appearance, their previous purchasing patterns, the type of clothes they're wearing, the type of car they drive, or anything else. You have to ask!

Here's how they do it at Uncle Bob's:

Bill: Mark, based on what you've told me so far, we have several types of boots that I think would work great for you. Let me ask you this, though. What is more important to you: making sure you get the best quality boots, or staying within a certain budget?

Customer: Well, to be honest with you, I don't want to spend too much. I'll only need these boots for a few hikes. I guess I would say I'm in the middle. I want to get the best boots, but I don't want to spend more than $100.

Bill: Not a problem! We can do that!

OR

Beth: Angie, as you can see, we have a huge selection to choose from, but I'm curious. What's the most important thing to you? Do you want to get the nicest dog house for your new puppy, or do you want to stay within a certain budget?

Customer: Look, I don't care about price! Little Princess is going to be a member of our family. She deserves the best!

Beth: Great! That gives us lots of options. Keep in mind, finding the *best* doghouse for Little Princess is my number one priority.

In both of these examples, a simple question saved the GREAT salesperson lots of time and energy. Bill won't be showing his customer the ultimate high-end hiking boots that retail for $595. He's clearly not interested. Beth knows she can concentrate on finding the perfect doghouse for Little Princess, without confining herself to selections limited by price.

Either way, the customers will be given options that clearly meet their wants and needs, because the salesperson listened to them. If you believe that the relationship is more important than the transaction, you can see that these two principles reinforce the customer's trust when we ask these price-oriented questions!

RICK SAYS

There's a new breed of customers out there. These customers have been raised knowing retailers play games with price. They've seen years of deep discounting by mega-chains, and as a result, no one trusts prices anymore! Now shopping has become a kind of sport — what can I get for the lowest price?

To counter this, you can ask questions centering on conditions of use. Conditions of use questions help determine where and under what conditions the customer plans on using their purchase.

Depending on what type of store you work in, this information can make a critical difference! The golf clubs you sell to the weekend duffer will be very different from the clubs you sell to the local semi-pro who hits the green five days a week!

CONDITIONS OF USE

Conditions of use questions are often the easiest, because they come very naturally.

Here are some examples of conditions of use questions:

Where do you work/sail/go dancing/work out/etc.?

Tell me about the type of work/exercise routine/crafts, etc. you do.

How often will you use _____?

How many hours at a time will you use _____?

Are you the only person who will be using _____, or will you be sharing it with family members/partner/co-workers?

Now, we've given you lots of sample questions. You're not going to ask all of them to every customer. You may also have questions in mind that don't appear on our list. The point is to generate a base of questions you can draw from, then select and customize questions to best suit the needs of each customer.

Remember to *listen* to the customer's answers. Make them the **focus** of your attention. Make **eye contact** — it really helps!

Remember to ask the customer's permission to ask questions! This strengthens your relationship with the customer and is a subtle form of compliment.

As a rule of thumb, the classier your store is, the more often you ask permission to ask questions.

Here's how they do it at Uncle Bob's:

Bonnie: So what part of your wardrobe are we working on today?

Customer: I need a new outfit for work. I need to freshen up my look.

Bonnie: Great! Let me ask you a few questions to make sure I put together the right solution for you. What do you do?

Customer: I'm a sales rep for the local TV station.

Bonnie: Okay, so is there a particular dress code you have to meet?

Customer: No, not really. We tend to be more casual, but we can't wear jeans and t-shirts, you know?

Bonnie: You said you want to freshen up your look. Can you tell me what you've been wearing?

Customer: Uh, usually I wear khakis and a polo shirt. Sometimes I wear a long sleeve shirt since I have to be out in the rain sometimes, especially when I travel.

Bonnie: Oh, travel. So you need something that will look good after you've been in the car awhile?

Customer: Absolutely! I hate looking all wrinkled and sweaty!

Bonnie: Do you have favorite colors?

Customer: Not really — but I hate green! I absolutely will not wear green.

Bonnie: Got it, no green. Are there any particular designers you favor?

Customer: Oh, I love Liz Claiborne.

Bonnie: Me too! Isn't she amazing? Excellent choice, especially for your body type!

Customer: I always get compliments when I wear her stuff.

Bonnie: Let me make sure I got this all correctly. You need an outfit for work that will wow your customers. It needs to be a fabric that stands up well to travel — and definitely not green! You like Liz Claiborne and her style, so we're looking for something simple yet classy. Did I miss anything, or is there anything else you would like to add?

Customer: No, I think you've got everything.

Bonnie: Okay, based on what you told me, there are a couple of outfits I think you'd just love. Just relax, and I'll be right back.

Did you see how Bonnie used her listening skills to **research** the customer's needs? She discovered lots of information about the customer's wants and needs in a relatively short time. And you better believe when she brings out some outfits for the customer, they won't be green!

Let's take a look at how things are going over in Uncle Bob's Exercise Equipment department:

Bill: So, Jenny, tell me about your exercise routine.

Customer: Well, I'm just kind of getting back into fitness, so right now I don't know if I'd call it a routine.

Bill: I understand perfectly! Let's try this: tell me where you are now, and where you'd like to be in say, six months?

Customer: Well, right now, I'm taking my bike out about two times a week. I'd like to get back to four, but it's been really difficult for me.

Bill: Okay. Could you tell me where you're running into problems?

Customer: Well, the place where I go biking is by our house. But that area's not as safe as it used to be. Some sketchy characters hang out there, especially once it gets dark.

Bill: So you're concerned about your safety?

Customer: Exactly! But I don't want to give up the biking. It's great cardio.

Bill: So you're looking for a way to enjoy the benefits of biking without compromising your safety. I think I've got a couple of ideas. But let me ask you some questions first, to help us find the ideal solution for your problem. Do you have space in your house for an exercise bike?

Customer: Not really. It's a small house, and I've got a lot of stuff . . .

Bill: Not a problem. We've got a line of portable trainers that you can use in your driveway or yard without taking up any valuable space in your house. We've got a wide range of trainers. Would you say it's more important to have the best trainer for your workouts, or do you have a budget we need to stick to?

Customer: I don't have a ton of money, but I wouldn't mind paying a little extra for a quality trainer. There's no sense buying junk!

Bill: You're right! So, just to make sure I've got everything, we're looking for a trainer that allows you to use your bike when you don't want to ride through the rough side of town. You want a quality piece of equipment, preferably one that doesn't take up a lot of space. Did I miss anything?

Customer: No, you got it.

Bill: Excellent! Why don't you follow me, and based on what you told me, I'll show you the trainers that would work best for you.

Complimenting the Customer Makes Them Like You

The RESEARCHING PHASE gives you a great opportunity to help the customer like you. You might have noticed that during the questioning, both Bonnie and Bill worked in some compliments.

Bonnie complimented her customer on liking Liz Claiborne and followed up with a secondary compliment that it wasn't surprising that the customer received compliments when she wore her designer of choice. This tells the customer that Bonnie respects her judgment — something everyone likes to hear!

Bill's compliments were a little more subtle. He said, "I understand perfectly" and "You're right!" Agreeing with the customer is a form of compliment. You're telling the customer that they're smart.

Don't be afraid of compliments. One sincere compliment can do marvels for your rapport with the customer. There are three primary areas to focus compliments on:

1. COMPLIMENT THEIR POSSESSIONS

Complimenting someone's possessions is easy.

"What a wonderful ring!"

"I have the same mower! Isn't it awesome?"

Complimenting a possession is a validation of the customer's judgment and taste. Almost everyone responds well to a compliment on their possessions.

2. COMPLIMENT THEIR PHYSICAL APPEARANCE

Complimenting a customer's physical appearance can be tricky. You really have to exercise your judgment here. However, there are some instances when it will work really well for the savvy salesperson:

> "I can tell you work out!" (Fitness stores)

> "That's a great designer for your body type!"

> "I love you hair color! It works so well with either silver or gold!"

3. COMPLIMENT THEIR DECISIONS

This is one area where we, as GREAT salespeople, can learn from every waiter and waitress working across this nation. What does a GREAT server say after you've placed your order?

> *"Excellent choice!"*

This is a compliment of your judgment — even if your judgment consisted of nothing more taxing than deciding on the surf 'n turf special! This compliment is one of the most powerful tools GREAT salespeople have at their disposal.

Other ways to compliment your customer's decisions:

"You know how to pick them!"

"What a smart buyer you are!"

"You've got a great eye!"

Another way to compliment a customer's decisions is to ask for their opinion.

For example, ask a regular customer, "You've got such a great eye! Can I show you the new line we just got in and get your opinion? I'd really love to see what you think!"

Special Bonus: Complimenting your customers cuts down on returns and helps eliminate buyer's remorse!

WRAPPING IT UP WITH THE SUMMARY

The last thing to do before moving on to the EXPERIMENTING PHASE is to summarize your research. This summary allows you to make sure you've heard everything the customer has said correctly.

Draw on your listening skills here.

Simply repeat back to the customer exactly what you've heard from them. Nothing will help them respect you more or build more confidence than this. It shows you listened!

It also provides the customer with an opportunity to refine their wants and needs and to clarify what they've said to you. Customers can and do make mistakes, so offering this opportunity to make everything clear is a service to both of you.

The summary builds confidence in you. At this point, it's pretty likely that you could recommend a product that isn't what they had in mind — but could very well be the best solution for their problem. For a customer to buy something totally other than what they'd imagined, they've really, really got to trust you.

When you finish the summary, ask a question such as "Have I missed anything?" or "Is there anything else I should know?"

If you have missed something, the customer will let you know. If you haven't missed anything, you, like the doctor, are ready to provide a solution. This is the EXPERI-MENTING PHASE, where you will present merchandise (solutions) to the customer.

Set the stage for the EXPERIMENTING PHASE with one of the most powerful phrases in sales:

"Based on what you told me...."

You're going to see that phrase come up time and time again once we move into the next phase. But let's take a quick moment now to talk about why "Based on what you told me . . ." is so effective.

Customers want to buy. They don't want to be sold.

When you use the phrase "Based on what you told me . . ." you're presenting the customer the opportunity to buy. In the customer's eyes, **this isn't selling. It's customer service**.

Think about it. When was the last time you heard someone say: "You have got to see the new shirt this guy sold me!"

Probably never, right? You're far more likely to hear something like this: "Look at this awesome shirt I just bought!"

Chapter 6 Review

→ Research is important because it:
> Makes it easy to bond with customers
> Makes it easy to suggest merchandise the customer will like
> Makes it easy to sell to the customer

→ Suggestions must meet the customer's Three A's (accurate, appropriate, appealing)

→ People come to a specialty store for a reason and your job is to discover what that reason is

→ Research means asking questions

→ Conduct research to help the customer identify and articulate their needs

→ Understand wants, needs, and be able to convert a want into a need

→ Listening is essential to your likeability

→ How to Listen:
> Face your customer
> Focus on customer's words
> Don't interrupt
> Encourage further conversation
> Mirror words

→ Three factors that influence your customers
> Past Experience
> New Expectations
> Conditions of Use

→ Price is not the most important thing

→ Make customers like you by using compliments on their:
Possessions
Physical Appearance
Decisions

→ Finish with a Summary

→ "Based on what you told me . . ."

Chapter 7

EXPERIMENTING AND CLOSING

e've moved through the GREETING PHASE and the RESEARCHING PHASE, and now it's time to enter the EXPERI-MENTING AND CLOSING PHASE. During this, we make suggestions to our customer. We experiment to see if what we offer appeals, or if we need to adjust our offerings to get the customer to buy.

Experimenting is a process of trial and error.

We try one piece of merchandise, and if that doesn't work for the customer, we try something else. There's one thing we absolutely have to keep in mind as we move into the EXPERIMENTING and CLOSING PHASE, and it's something we've already discussed (let's see if you remember):

Logic makes us shop. Emotion makes us buy.

The key to selling is to focus on the things that interest the customer. To your customer, guess what the most important thing in the world is?

It's not price.

It's not quality.

It's not style.

It's not selection.

The most important thing to a customer is: the customer! Every customer wants to know one thing:

"What's in it for me?"

While customers may try to convince you (and themselves) that they make purchasing decisions based upon rock-solid logic, the truth of the matter is the major influence on any purchase is the answer to this question:

"How will buying this make me FEEL?"

Your job is to ensure a **positive answer**. If buying it will make your customer feel . . .

Good

Attractive

Smart

Sharp

Savvy

Wise

Responsible

Stylish

Generous

Sexy

. . . they're going to buy.

However, if the answer to that question is any of the following negative words . . .

Trapped

Tricked

Pressured

Manipulated

Scammed

Resentful

Stupid

Foolish

Wasteful

Insecure

. . . they're not going to buy. Even worse, they'll feel they've **been sold**.

> **Customers who feel they've been sold will:**
>
> *Not be happy with their purchase*
>
> *Be more likely to return the merchandise*
>
> *Tell their friends about the bad experience they had*
>
> *Not return to your store*

We want our customers to be happy and we want them to come back. The lifetime value of any one customer is many times greater than any one purchase they might make. The longer someone shops in our store, the more likely they are to buy.

That's the point of the EXPERIMENTING and CLOSING PHASE. We want to help customers reach their goal, whatever that may be. This is the point where we're going to demonstrate our concern for the customer. This is where we're going to show them *"What's in it for them."*

What Do Customers Want To See?

Customers want to see three things:

1. A solution to their stated need or problem

2. A product that reinforces their self-image

3. At a price they're willing to pay

Let's look at each of these in turn.

1. A SOLUTION TO THEIR STATED NEED OR PROBLEM

At this point in the sale, you should be focusing on presenting the customer with options that will address the needs and problems you discovered during the RESEARCHING PHASE.

This is where all of your active listening skills kick in. By combining the information you gathered with your product knowledge you should be able to select options from your merchandise that fulfill the customer's needs.

Be careful!
This is where many, many, many, many, many, many sales professionals go astray.

Why? They don't show the customer what the customer wants. They show the customer what they think the customer should have.

We know it's tempting. It's so easy to pull the dress that "everybody's buying" or the stereo that's hot and new and heavily promoted. But that is not helping your customer!

Some customers don't want the dress everyone's buying.

Some customers don't want the stereo that's hot and new and heavily promoted.

It is not our job to decide what the customer wants. That is the customer's job! There is no rule that says what they want is right or wrong — it's just what they want!

The point of experimenting is to find the merchandise that meet the customer's needs or solves the customer's problems. Bear in mind that these items may not actually be the merchandise the customer winds up buying. Or your suggestions may be only one or two items in a multi-purchase sale. But we'll talk more about that later.

2. PRODUCTS THAT REINFORCE SELF-IMAGE

There are two parts of every transaction: the **business part** and the **human part**.

The **business part** includes showing the customer merchandise that meets their needs, at a price they're willing to pay.

Reinforcing the customer's self-image is the **human part** of the transaction. This is the fun side of selling! This is when you "read" your customer and help them find merchandise that will make them feel absolutely fantastic.

The best lines you can use appeal directly to reinforcing the customer's self-image:

The Customer's Self-Image	How You Reinforce It
Fun-loving and Spontaneous	Let's go play!
Super Genius	I'd love your opinion on . . .
Status Seeker	Here is our very best . . .
	Everyone's buying . . .
Insecure/Nervous	Let's go try this . . .
The Director	I can tell you know what you want. It's over here . . .

The Golden Rule tells us that we should treat people the way we want to be treated. To be a GREAT salesperson, we need to take things to a higher level. We need to embrace the **Platinum Rule**!

The Platinum Rule, developed by Dr. Tony Allesandro, goes like this:

> *Treat customers the way THEY want to be treated!*

3. A PRICE THEY'RE WILLING TO PAY

Price is just a number. Many times retailers try to find the **magic price** — the price their customers won't be able to resist.

We hate to tell you, but the magic price doesn't exist. There is merchandise in this world that your customer will never buy, whether it's at a fair price, sold at cost, or even sold below cost!

Why?

Because they don't want it! Or, more importantly, they don't see the value in the purchase. No matter how much (or little) they are willing to spend, they don't see the benefit of owning that particular piece of merchandise.

Right now you want the customer to see the value in the options you're showing them. This means focusing on benefits.

Benefits Add Value. Features Add Cost.

The retail price of an item will always be too expensive or too high in the customer's mind until they see the value. This means understanding the benefits.

Benefits answer the question, "What's in it for me?" Or in other words, what owning this product will do for them and their self-esteem.

UNDERSTANDING BENEFITS = UNDERSTANDING VALUE

Presenting value tips the scales in your favor.

If the perceived value of a product (and perceived value is just a shorthand way to say "How much the customer thinks the merchandise is worth") is less than the price, the customer will never, ever, ever buy.

If the perceived value is equal to the price, the customer will have to think it over and you'll have your work cut out for you.

But if the perceived value is greater than the price, the customer will buy!

UNDERSTANDING BENEFITS AND FEATURES

Benefits and features play a pivotal role in your success as a GREAT salesperson. But before we talk about how you can use benefits and features to generate more sales, let's make sure everyone understands what benefits are and what features are — and the difference between the two.

> **Feature.** A physical part or characteristic of the merchandise.

> **Benefit.** The value derived from a particular feature.

YOUR MISSION

The biggest challenge you have as a GREAT sales professional is informing the customer about the features of the merchandise in such a way that they see the value of the options you are presenting.

And if we think back just a few paragraphs, we'll remember:

Understanding Benefits = Understanding Value

For a customer to see the value, you must offer solid **benefit statements**.

Benefit statements:

Are easy to remember

Highlight your product knowledge

Are easy to understand

Creating benefits statements is easy. Every time you want the customer to understand the value of a particular feature, you simply say:

This has (feature) **which means** (benefits).

Because this product has (feature) **you'll be able to** (benefit).

Do you see this (feature)? **That means that** (benefit).

Using these simple sentences, you can show the customer the answer to their #1 question: "What's in it for me?"

You can use benefit statements to transform any feature into a true benefit for the customer.

Here's how they do it at Uncle Bob's:

Bonnie: This hiking boot has a Gore-Tex® lining. That means your feet stay dry in wet conditions, because the Gore-Tex® lining shields out 99.5 percent of the water.

Bill: This snow blower has an easily adjustable chute. That means you can keep your neighbors happy, because you can keep the snow you're blowing out of your driveway out of their driveway!

Beth: This watch features a durable Swiss precision movement. This means it's always accurate, and you'll never be late to a sales appointment. Nothing makes a client angrier than having to wait, am I right?

Remember that we are focusing on what the customer will receive as a result of the feature we're discussing. Different customers will want different things from the merchandise you're showing. You have to identify if they're looking for an **emotional benefit** or a **mechanical benefit**.

Emotional Benefits vs. Mechanical Benefits

An emotional benefit is how the merchandise makes you feel. Does it make you feel sexy, smart, happy, etc? Most customers are looking for the emotional benefit.

A mechanical benefit is how does this merchandise function better than other, similar merchandise? This type of benefit is of primary interest to the analytical customer. Analytical customers thrive on facts and data. They want every bit of information you can give them. Note: This is a small group of customers who you can usually identify by the type of questions they ask.

Each of the examples highlighted above focuses on a specific benefit the customer could expect to enjoy if they make the purchase:

Dry, comfortable feet

Happy neighbors and effective snow removal

Increased sales due to timeliness

Notice there's no guarantee in the third example. In fact, Beth never explicitly states that the customer will sell more to his clients by wearing the watch. However, she does say that the customer will be on time, which makes for happy clients. The implication is clear: happy clients buy! Here the benefit statement focuses on hoped-for results!

Remember: Features tell. Benefits sell!

GREAT Benefit Statements

As you practice G.R.E.A.T. Selling, you'll quickly get the hang of creating GREAT benefit statements. You'll learn to think in terms of benefit statements. You won't be able to look at a piece of merchandise without thinking "How will this **benefit** my customers?"

Common benefits include:

Saving time

Saving money

Saving the planet

Appropriate

Understated

Popular

THE DANGER ZONE

You're selling merchandise, not auditioning for the show "How It's Made"!

Too many people get caught up in "how the feature works" and not "what the feature does." Part of your role here is as an interpreter, particularly if you sell merchandise with features that are very technical and confusing.

Explaining how the feature works may not help at all. It might even lose your sale! Overwhelming your customer with technical information will confuse them. And the more confused your customer is, the less likely they are to buy.

Don't give too much information at once. Space it out throughout the conversation.

Always focus your benefit statements on the issues you discovered during the RESEARCHING PHASE. Mention those benefits first and often.

WHEN TO USE BENEFIT STATEMENTS

Every customer is different. Every store is different. Every sale is different. That makes it tricky to say: This is the exact right time to use benefit statements. Don't feel bound to follow our example letter for letter.

In fact, many customers are very short on time. Over-packed schedules mean that every minute counts! Your ability to multi-task and deliver benefit statements while experimenting will become very valuable to you. The more you practice this, the easier it will become!

Asking For The Sale

You've come a long way with your customer. You've GREETED them, RESEARCHED them, and now you've EXPERIMENTED.

Guess what? It's at this point most salespeople stop! You can almost see them do it. They've gone through the motions to this point and then they freeze up. They come to a grinding halt — just when it is time to ask for the sale!

To complete the sale, you have to ask the customer to buy!

HOW DO YOU KNOW WHEN TO CLOSE A SALE?

There are certain signs or signals that we look for — verbal and non-verbal signs. First let's examine the **verbal signals**. When a customer says any of the following we know it is a verbal sign to start closing the sale.

"I really like this one."

"How much is it?"

"This really feels good."

"This just feels right."

"I see what you mean."

"Good suggestion."

"This is just what I was looking for."

"This goes great with _____."

"Do you deliver?"

Now here are the **non-verbal signs** it's time to start closing the sale:

When the customer is smiling

When they touch or hold the merchandise

When they are nodding their head in approval

When they start to demonstrate excited body posture

When you see them grabbing their cell phone to call family or friends

When any of these verbal or non-verbal signs occur, start closing that sale and make sure that item is solidly sold.

A common error is when a salesperson starts to suggest an add-on item before the first item is a completed sale.

When you start to make another suggestion without tying up the loose end first, you are running the risk of losing the initial sale. Make sure the first item is sold before attempting any add-ons. Having said that, it doesn't mean you have to technically ring up a sale. But you do have to feel secure that the item is sold.

The next step in closing the sale is the use of "tie-downs."

Tips To Tie Down The Sale

After you have given a benefit statement, you need to make sure the customer understood it. If your customer doesn't understand the benefit statement, it is useless!

How do you make sure the customer understands? You use **tie-down statements.**

A tie-down is a statement designed to gather agreement from the customer.

You want to make sure the customer understands the benefit statement, and more importantly, that they agree with it. A tie-down is hung at the end of a sentence. For example:

"Since you hike in some very muddy areas, hiking boots that can keep your feet dry are very important to you, aren't they?"

If what you have said represents the truth as the customer sees it, then they will respond by agreeing with you. When they agree that the benefit statement you have just given meets their needs, they are moving closer to buying, aren't they?

THE TOP TEN TIE-DOWN STATEMENTS OF ALL TIME

Aren't you?

Don't you?

Isn't it?

Can't you?

Didn't it?

Won't you?

Doesn't it?

Aren't they?

Wouldn't it?

Don't you think?

Let's look at how they do it at Uncle Bob's, starting with benefit statements and working right through to the tie-down:

Bonnie: Based on what you've told me, I think we have the perfect phone for your mother. This model features oversized, well-spaced buttons, which means they're easy to see and use — even with arthritic fingers!

Customer: It does look easy to use.

Bonnie: You're right! It's very simple to operate. And the volume control is right here, so your mother can easily adjust it to make sure she hears every word. We don't want her to miss out on anything, do we?

Customer: No, she hates not being able to hear. This looks like a phone she'll actually use!

OR

Bill: Now, you said you travel a lot for your company, correct?

Customer: That's right.

Bill: That's why I think you might appreciate this briefcase. It features an RIFD microchip, which means that if anyone steals your bag, it can easily be traced and recovered. This system works throughout North America and Northern Europe, which is where you do the lion's share of your traveling — am I right?

Customer: Yes, you are. So this bag can be tracked no matter where the thief goes?

Bill: Within North America and Northern Europe, absolutely. And let me show you this — this works worldwide! The integrated locking system means that no one, absolutely no one, can open the bag without first entering your security code. They could use a hacksaw, a blow torch, you name it, but they're not getting into your bag without the code. That type of security is important to you, isn't it?

Customer: Absolutely!

G.R.E.A.T. Selling works in every part of the store, in every department, in every category. It works if you sell lawn tractors. It works if you sell fine jewelry. It works if you sell prom dresses. It works if you sell chainsaws.

A **tie-down** is a way to gently direct the customer to agree with the positive benefits of the product. You want the customer to agree with you and simply say "yes."

How to Handle Objections

Part of closing a sale is answering objections.

Rule #1 when a customer makes an objection is to always compliment them on their objection! Do this by simply saying something like:

"You bring up a good point."

"That's a good idea, I am glad you said that."

"I didn't think of that, let's discuss it."

Remember that customers go out to shop because it feels good. Shopping is a feel-good experience.

When a customer disagrees with something, they might be expecting some type of confrontation. When you compliment their objection you diffuse any possible minor hostilities.

THE FOUR "F'S"

One of the best techniques to use in overcoming objections is a technique referred to as the four "F's." They stand for **feel – felt – found – felt**. The four "F's" are used when the customer is confused or not quite ready to make a commitment (of course you could be dealing with that "wishy-washy" customer who is **always** afraid to make a decision). This is how it goes: "I know how you **feel** about making a big decision about buying this _____. I **felt** the same way, but I **found** (here's a place you can use your own experience to relate with the customer). After I made the decision I really **felt** so much better."

Sometimes by just asking that you can come back with a rebuttal, but if nothing else you are able to better understand the customer. If a particular objection continues to keep coming up, it is something that must be addressed at the store. When a customer says, "The prices are too high" you make a suggestion of looking at a less expensive item. Whatever you do, **do not start negotiating price** with the customer at this point! You might have to adjust the price later on, but this is not the place to do it.

When the customer says, "I want to think it over," your next line should be: "Excellent idea! Now tell me exactly what you want to think over." By just asking that, sometimes you can reveal the true reasons why they are not buying. Even if this doesn't help in making the sale, it will give you valuable information about various products. When a customer objects to the product, take the path of least resistance and simply show them another product. If you know the original product is the best option, don't be afraid to re-introduce that product again later in the sale.

When does a salesperson become a salesperson? When the customer says "No."

Sometimes we need to just make the decision for the customer when they are afraid to make a commitment. We step forward and say, **"This is what we're going to do."**

When a customer is being unreasonable the line to use is "I wish we could."

When the customer says, "It's not in the budget," smile or chuckle a little and say, "A budget is only an estimate. Some things you're going to be higher on and some things you are going to be lower on. In this case you are a little higher."

Specialty businesses generally close 40 to 50 percent of the customers who come into the store.

That's why we should always assume that the customer **is** going to be buying and proceed with closing the sale, especially when you have answered all of their wants and needs.

THE BENJAMIN FRANKLIN

One of the classic types of closing techniques is referred to as *The Benjamin Franklin.* Take a clean sheet of paper and draw a line down the middle. Put the pros of the purchase on one side and the cons on the other. Make sure you show more reasons to buy than not to buy!

FOR STATUS-SEEKERS

The last type of close is specifically designed for the status-seeking customer. You simply use the line "everybody's buying it." For some people, keeping up with what is hot and trendy is the most important thing. Just be careful where you use this line. Remember, closing the sale should be as natural as possible. The goal is to sell people what they want or need, even if they don't realize that they want or need it.

Chapter 7 Review

→ Experimenting is a process of trial and error

→ Logic makes us shop. Emotion makes us buy.

→ The most important thing to a customer is:
the customer

→ Customers want to see three things:
A solution to their stated need or problem
A product that reinforces their self-image
At a price they're willing to pay

→ Products that reinforce self-image

→ The **business part**: showing the customer
merchandise that meets their needs, at a price
they're willing to pay

→ The **human part**: reinforcing the customer's
self-image

→ Follow the Platinum Rule: Treat customers the
way **they** want to be treated

→ A price the customer is willing to pay

→ Benefits add value. Features add cost.

→ Use benefit statements

→ Emotional benefits vs. mechanical benefits

- Look for the signs and the signals to start closing the sale
  - Verbal signs
  - Non-verbal signs

- Using tie-down statements

- Complimenting the objection

- The four "F's" feel – felt – found – felt

- Make the decision

- Price objections

- Product objections

- "Let me think it over"

- "It's not in the budget"

- The Ben Franklin

- For status seekers: "Everybody's buying it"

Chapter 8
ADD-ONS

ow! We're moving right along here. It's time to talk about the "A" in G.R.E.A.T. Selling: **Add-Ons.**

Add-Ons are, in our opinion, the really fun part of selling. At this point, you've made the first sale. Now it's time to see what else you can get the customer to buy!

Would you like to know a secret? It's a secret your bosses already know. Understanding this secret will not only make you a GREAT salesperson, it's going to make you more valuable to your store. Remember all that stuff we said about job security and better commissions?

It all hinges on this secret.

Stores don't make their money on the first item any customer purchases.

They make a little profit, sure. But a lot of that profit gets eaten up taking care of overhead, advertising, paying salespeople — all that stuff that explains why your manager looks stressed out so often.

The real money comes from the second item the customer purchases — or the third, the fourth or even fifth. The more you can sell to any one customer, the more money your store is going to make.

Not only that, but the more you sell a customer, the happier that customer is going to be! There are few things that make a shopper as happy as walking into a store, intending to look around or "maybe" buy one thing, and walking out a little while later, absolutely loaded down with bulging shopping bags!

It's fun, plain and simple. As shopping has become entertainment, you've made the customer happy by showing them a good time!

In this section, we're going to talk about **additions**, or how to get the customer to **buy more** and **be happy**.

Fair Warning: In this chapter, you're going to find the **four magic words** that will absolutely transform your life as a sales professional. These four magic words are so powerful that they can even be used by people who don't speak the language! You'll read more about that later. We just want you to be fully prepared, because you're going to start selling a lot more merchandise — starting today!

How to Sell Add-Ons

Add-ons come in two varieties. A customer can buy merchandise from **an extra category** or they can **accessorize** their original purchase.

Which one's better?

That depends. Which is better, a hot fudge sundae or lemon meringue pie? Which one would you rather have, a vintage Harley Davidson or a shiny new Corvette? Would you rather have a partner who is smart or sexy?

In other words, it's all good! You don't have to make a choice. If the customer adds on an item from another category or they add on by accessorizing, either way, you win!

To make it even better, they could do both!

But before we go into how this all works, let's look at some definitions.

The Extra Category. Offering additions from an extra category means showing the customer something very similar to what they've just purchased, but slightly different. For example, if the customer has just purchased a pair of running shoes, maybe they'd be interested in hiking boots, or high heels, or sandals, or a pair of slippers. You're still in footwear, clearly, but you've moved on to another type of footwear.

Accessorizing. To accessorize, you offer the customer additions that "go with" the first item they've purchased. For example, if your customer has just picked out a great dress, she's going to want jewelry and stockings and shoes and hair ornaments and a shawl to go with it. Get this picture? In this type of addition, you're helping the customer more fully enjoy their initial purchase by providing add-on accessories that complete the outfit.

ADDING THE EXTRA CATEGORY

You can't have too much of a good thing! That's the logic behind adding an extra category. Your customer has already committed to one purchase from your store. Now you're going to show them something completely different (but similar) — that makes the customer happy!

Adding an extra category can be great customer service!

When a customer buys many items, from a range of categories, they'll have a lot of options available to them. If you're in apparel, this means every time your customer goes to the closet, they'll have lots of outfits to choose from. If you're a jeweler, your customer will have more pieces in their jewelry box, allowing them to complement a wider range of clothes. If you're in hardware, your customer will not only have every tool they need, they'll have a handy toolbox to keep everything organized.

You're helping your customer be prepared!

Here's a GREAT line you can use to add an extra category to your sale:

great 4 access.

"Let's play!"

Customers love to have fun. Once they've gotten through the "business" part of the shopping trip — they've picked out and purchased the item they came to your store for — they can relax and enjoy themselves.

Here's how it works at Uncle Bob's:

Bonnie: Excellent! Now that we've gotten the outfit you need for work all picked out, are you ready to have a little fun? We've just gotten a new line of sundresses in that I think you would love. Let's just try one on you and see how it looks!

Bill: Do you want to see something cool? I know you came in for your laptop battery, but you won't want to miss this hot new game!

Always, always, always pull an extra category (or two) when you're showing merchandise.

These don't have to be the first thing you show the customer. Clearly you want to focus on the first sale first. But you want to have it readily available when it's time to have fun.

If the customer asks about the extra category item, simply smile and say:

"I couldn't resist! Isn't this great? I thought you'd love it, especially since you're so _____ !" (Fill in the blank with whatever word works best.)

Smart

Stylish

Trendy

Handy

⌒ *a random* GREAT *idea* ⌒

Sometimes you don't need an extra category.
Sometimes you need another color!

For example:

Bonnie: These turtlenecks are so comfortable. I brought the blue and red out too, just in case . . .

Bill: The nice thing about these boots is they come in black and brown, so you can wear them with anything.

➤ *another random* GREAT *idea* ➤

Have the customer try it on!

The smartest, easiest way to get a customer to say "yes" to merchandise is to have them interact with it. How does this work? Like this:

Bonnie: Just for fun, why don't you try this on? The color's fabulous.

Bill: You'd never believe how much fun this game is. Here, give it a shot.

This strategy is particularly effective with the "Belonging" and "Director" customer types. You can almost guarantee they won't be able to resist this approach.

Beth: Since you're here, would you mind just trying on this jacket? I'd love to have your opinion.

Bill: We just got these in. Do you think they're going to appeal to our customers?

Notice that these sentences are **compliments**. They make the customer feel **valued** and **important.**

Accessorizing

We're going to start this section off with a little exercise. Are you ready?

Think about the last time you went to the grocery store. You might have headed there with a short list in mind. Maybe you needed milk, bread and some juice boxes for your daughter's lunchbox.

But when you got to the grocery store, bananas were on sale, so you picked up a bunch. Then there were these awesome rotisserie chickens, and they smelled so good, you couldn't resist. Then you grabbed your bread. On your way to the milk, you passed a display full of tuna — 6 cans for $5! So you loaded up the cart. Standing at the milk cooler, you noticed some fresh cut flowers, and that reminded you that you needed a birthday card for your boss. So off you went to the card aisle. Then you grabbed some toothpaste, a pack of gum, and a copy of *People* magazine.

It was only after you got home that you realized, as you unloaded the milk and bread, there were no juice boxes anywhere in sight!

How did you feel when you had to go back out to get the juice boxes? Pretty stupid, that's how.

That's the feeling we want to avoid when we help our customers accessorize!

Let's look at why the grocery store scenario happens. Logically, it shouldn't. You went into the store knowing what you wanted. You even had a list! Yet you walked out with only some of what you wanted, along with lots of things you didn't know you wanted.

The reason you left the grocery store with things you didn't know you wanted is because the store did a good job distracting you from your primary purpose, enticing you with irresistible merchandise. The deals were too good to pass up — so you didn't!

But all these great deals did not make you happy.

Why? **Because you didn't get the juice boxes!**

If we're going to have happy customers, we need to provide the juice boxes (the customer's original want or need), as well as the extra stuff they didn't even know they wanted when they came in.

It is your job as a salesperson, as a GREAT salesperson, to ensure the customer gets what they want — as well as the extras!

Whenever you make a sale, the first question you should be asking yourself is:

"What does the customer need to go with this?"

Never assume:

That the customer has what they need

That the customer knows what they need

That the customer wouldn't want what they need, if offered

Instead, assume that the customer:

Doesn't have what they need

Probably doesn't know they need it

Would be happy if they had it to enhance their enjoyment of their new purchase

And once again, we go back to a technique we've been using all along: **We ask!**

Simple questions at this point can help your customer get full enjoyment from their purchase. Bear in mind that your customers aren't going to see this as selling. **You're simply taking care of their needs. That's not selling. That's customer service!**

Here's how it works at Uncle Bob's:

Bonnie: Now, you can charge this cell phone in your car or in your house. What kind of charger would you prefer?

Bill: You'll need a cleaning kit for your rifle. Do you prefer the compact kit, or this larger kit you can use for all your guns?

ACCESSORIZING WITHOUT ASKING

You can add on accessories without asking. And there are definitely times when this is actually the best option.

How do you do this? Simply by showing more merchandise!

Here are some GREAT ways to do this:

Here's the _____ that goes with that _____.

This _____ would be perfect with your new _____, don't you agree?

You'll need _____ in order to _____.

Do you have a _____? You'll want one for your new _____.

To take care of your new _____, you need _____.

Here's how it works at Uncle Bob's:

Bonnie: You've just got to try these earrings! They go perfectly with that dress!

Bill: You'll need these shear pins to go with your snow blower.

Beth: Have you tried that new sunscreen everyone's talking about? You'll definitely want some when you're wearing that great new swimsuit!

These strategies work — not every time, but a good portion of the time. If you try them with every customer, and they work 25 percent of the time, your sales numbers are going to go through the roof!

And that's not all. You have another tool at your disposal. This strategy is so very, very powerful that it will shock you. This is a technique that works in every type of store, for every salesperson, everywhere.

> *RICK SAYS*
>
> *This strategy even works if you don't speak English. I had an employee in one of my stores who only spoke Spanish, yet he mastered this phrase. And with this, and this alone, he turned in pretty decent sales numbers, month after month after month!*
>
> *What makes this even more remarkable is the fact that my Spanish-speaking employee wasn't even a salesman! He was the porter, hired to carry packages out to our customers' cars for them!*

These are **the four magic words** we mentioned at the beginning of this chapter. They are so powerful, and they're so easy to learn, that you can master them in less than a minute. I call this the sixty-second selling course:

Did you see this?

That's it! And here's how it works. You're walking through the store, either with a customer or passing by a customer on your way to another spot. All you have to do is stop and point at a piece of merchandise and say the magic words:

"Did you see this?"

And then you keep moving. You don't have to say another word. This is not the time to launch into a sales pitch or to point out benefits. You simply direct the customer's attention to the merchandise — and then you keep going about your business!

WHY "DID YOU SEE THIS?" WORKS

Why are these four words more effective than almost any other words you can use on the sales floor? What's so magical about the phrase "Did you see this?"

It creates curiosity — the customer wants to see what you thought was so great.

It focuses the customer's attention on one item.

It's suggestive selling.

There's absolutely no pressure on the customer.

It creates an inclusive atmosphere — the customer feels like they "belong."

It's easy to do.

HOW TO USE "DID YOU SEE THIS?"

The trick to "Did you see this?" is to use it often! Ask every customer if they've seen an item besides the one you've initially shown them.

You can use "Did you see this?" to point out:

New merchandise

Merchandise you think will appeal to that particular customer

Merchandise that's on sale

Best-selling merchandise

Keep asking "Did you see this?" until the customer lets you know they're done buying! This simple question can easily transform a single-item order into a multiple-piece purchase.

Rules for Add-Ons

1. Every sale should consist of more than one item
2. Keep adding until the customer says they're done
3. Never introduce a second item until you've closed on the first
4. Start adding while you're on the sales floor — don't wait until you're at the register

At this point, you've helped your customer find the right merchandise.

You've helped them find not only what they came in for, but things they didn't even know they wanted.

You kept asking "Did you see this?" until they'd seen it all.

They've got their wallet out and are ready to pay.

Are you done?

Not exactly!

Remember, the customer might have a lot of **fear and anxiety** about their purchase. They may not be sure they've picked out exactly the right merchandise. They might be freaking out about how much money they're spending.

This anxiety and fear combine to form a condition known as buyer's remorse.

A customer experiencing buyer's remorse is sad they've purchased something that they should not have bought.

Here's what happens when a customer has buyer's remorse:

They're not happy with their purchase.

They may return the item.

They feel like they've made a bad decision.

They are likely not to return to your store.

That's why it is imperative that you do everything you can to help the customer avoid buyer's remorse.

AVOIDING BUYER'S REMORSE

Lots of what you've already learned comes into this "do everything you can" category. The RESEARCHING PHASE is essential. You're listening to the customer and helping them find merchandise that fills their wants and needs. You're helping the customer make a GREAT purchase.

However, that isn't always enough to make the customer confident. Sometimes you have a customer who is nervous about their decision, for whatever reason.

That's why it is a good idea to **lock in the sale.**

Ways to Lock In the Sale

To lock in the sale you confirm that the customer made a GREAT decision. This is a combination of a **compliment** and **reassurance**.

THE COMPLIMENT

Remember, compliments are powerful. Everyone likes to hear nice things about themselves! You can use a compliment at this point to let the customer know they're:

Smart

Stylish

An informed shopper

A favorite customer

THE REASSURANCE

The reassurance part of locking in the sale is to help the customer feel like they made the absolute right choice. They're nervous. You want to alleviate that anxiety. You want to remove any doubt — because as long as the customer has any doubt, they're not going to be happy.

You can provide reassurance with **positive statements**. For example:

> *Those boots will be so comfortable!*
>
> *You're going to look great in this dress!*
>
> *You'll be able to take some amazing photos with your new camera!*

> **Use positive statements that address**
> **the customer's hopes.**

During the RESEARCHING PHASE, you should have discovered what the customer wants, needs and desires. This is the time to return to those wants, needs and desires.

Let the customer know that they've made a decision that will allow them to meet their wants, needs and desires.

Here's how they do it at Uncle Bob's:

Bonnie: I have to say it: you've made a really great decision today. You're going to love these boots! I want you to know, if you have any questions or concerns, I'm here Tuesday through Saturday from 10:00 A.M. to 6:00 P.M.

Bill: You are a really smart shopper. Buying this snow blower now, before the fall rush, is going to save you hundreds of dollars! And if we get an early storm the way we did last year, you'll be more than ready.

Beth: Your mother is absolutely going to love this telephone. It's just perfect. It is so sweet and loving of you to be so helpful.

Chapter 8 Review

→ Add-ons come in two varieties:
    Extra Category
    Accessorize

→ Compliments make add-ons possible

→ Always ask: *What does the customer need to go with this item?*

→ Never assume

→ The four magic words: Did you see this?

→ Prevent buyer's remorse

→ Lock in every sale with compliments and reassurance

Chapter 9

TETHERING

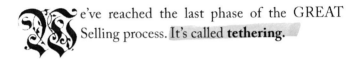

e've reached the last phase of the GREAT Selling process. It's called **tethering.**

What Is a Tether?

A tether is a connection. It's something that attaches you to your customer. It's a type of bond, a way you can reach out to your customer time and time again.

Remember, there's a lot of competition for your customer's attention.

There's the Internet and television, other stores, other activities, work, family — dozens and dozens of ways your customer could spend their time, energy, and money besides in your store.

If we want the customer to come back to us, we have to put some effort and energy into the relationship. We have to reach out to the customer and build a relationship.

In this section, we're going to focus on creating a tether with the customer. This means using tools and techniques to forge a strong relationship, so they'll want to come back, again and again and again!

In short, creating a tether gives you a way to stay in touch with the customer.

Staying In Touch

Why is staying in touch so important?

For a minute, we want you to think about what it takes to get a new customer to come into the store. Those buyers don't just magically wander in. A lot of times, energy and money help to attract customers.

Think about it. To attract customers, a store might do any or all of the following:

Radio advertising

Newspaper advertising

Magazine advertising

Online advertising

Sponsor community events

Run contests, sales or promotional events

Participate in community events

Put up billboard signage

Put a sign up in the parking lot or plaza entrance

Put signs and banners on the store

You might even have other ideas about how to draw customers to your store. If you do, we encourage you to share them with your manager or owner. There are never enough good promotional ideas — and there can never be too many new customers coming in!

What do all these ideas have in common? Two things:

1. They're all designed to draw new customers into the store.

2. They all cost money!

Retail research tells us that attracting a new customer is six to seven times more expensive than reaching out to an existing customer.

Think about it in terms of your workload. Who is easier to sell to?

• A customer who has never, ever been in your store before

• A regular customer who comes in all the time and loves the store

That's a no-brainer, isn't it? In "scientific retailing" terms, we call that a "No duh!"

It is easier and economically smarter for most retailers to sell to an existing customer than a new customer. That leaves you with one big question:

How Do You Make Existing Customers Come Back?

There is only one really proven, effective way to keep the customer coming back, time after time. You need to keep in touch with them and reach out to them regularly.

A store has a number of ways to reach out to customers:

E-mail

E-newsletters

Cell phone alerts

Phone calls

Direct mail

But to make these things work, you need contact information. You can't call someone if you don't know their phone number! You can't e-mail someone without an e-mail address.

Now, your store doesn't want to contact customers all the time. That's really expensive, and worse than that, if you're contacting customers about stuff that's not of interest to them, they're going to feel like you're pestering them and that can turn them off.

Instead, you want to contact customers only when you have news that the customer is likely to be interested in.

For example:

A women's apparel store calls all its customers who go on cruises when the new spring line comes in.

A ski shop e-mails all customers who snowboard when they are having a blowout mega sale.

A beautiful, arty postcard, addressed to a jeweler's very best customers, invites them to a special showing of a designer's newest pieces.

Because these messages are of interest to the customer, focusing on merchandise and events they are known to enjoy, the customer doesn't view the messages as advertising.

They see them as service.

THE VALUE OF CUSTOMER DATA

What does customer data include? Simply, it's everything you're going to want to know about the customer:

Name

Address

Home Phone Number

Work Phone Number

Cell Phone Number

E-mail Address

Preferred Way to Contact (cell phone, e-mail, home phone)

What type of merchandise they like to purchase

Type of customer they are (regular customer, incentive customer, sale customer, etc.)

Now, this sounds like a lot of information to keep track of, and quite frankly, it is.

But relax! Chances are most of this is not going to be your job.

Stores track customer data in a number of ways. One of the most common is the **preferred customer card**. These cards have a number of names. You'll also hear them called:

Loyalty cards

Frequent buyer cards

Savings cards

Club cards

It doesn't matter what the name is. What matters is that you get customers to sign up for the card and remind them to use it each and every time they shop. This allows your store's computers to track their buying patterns. Tracking makes it easier for your store to design events and sales that will appeal to the customer.

Here's how they get customers to sign up for Uncle Bob's Super Savings Card:

Bonnie: And your total is $37.79. Do you have an Uncle Bob's card?

Customer: No, I don't.

Bonnie: (taking out the easy-to-fill-out application) Well, here! Sign up and we'll send you coupons for the items you like to buy. And you'll save ten percent on today's purchase!

Did you notice what Bonnie **didn't** do? She **didn't ask** if the customer wanted an Uncle Bob's card. She assumed the customer would, and presented it to him with a **benefit statement**:

"Sign up and we'll send you coupons for the items you like to buy."

That's exactly what you need to do. **Focus on the benefits and assume they want it**!

⤜ *a random* GREAT *idea* ⤛

Ask your customers for their loyalty card each and every time they shop with you.

By asking your customers for their loyalty cards, you're help-ing to build the following aspects of their customer profile:

The type of merchandise they like to buy.

What type of customer they are.

Loyalty cards can also make the following parts of your life easier:

Returns

Exchanges

Why? Because all the information you'll need is stored in the computer. This is an added level of customer service. Why? As we all know, customers can and do lose receipts and other vital paperwork from time to time. If you've cap-tured the customer's purchase in the computer for them, you'll be able to work around that loss — and **keep your customer happy**!

Five Things You Need to Know About Customer Data Collection

1. Every customer's data is important, from the big spender to the bargain hunter.

2. Assume the customer will want a preferred customer card.

3. Focus on the benefits to the customer when you sign them up (coupons, frequent purchase discounts, savings, special events, etc.).

4. Assure the customer you'll only be contacting them with relevant offers.

5. Make sure customer data is kept confidential and treated with respect.

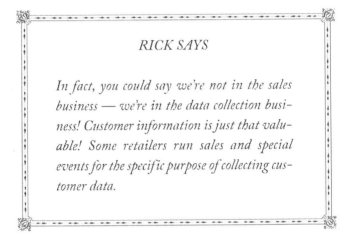

RICK SAYS

In fact, you could say we're not in the sales business — we're in the data collection business! Customer information is just that valuable! Some retailers run sales and special events for the specific purpose of collecting customer data.

What Happens to All This Customer Information?

Now that you understand what type of customer data stores want to collect, you may wonder what happens with all this information.

Every store is different. Each store will have its own unique promotional strategy. We can't say definitively what your store is doing with its customer information, but here are some common strategies:

Send customers thank you cards

Make follow-up calls to make sure the customer is happy with their purchase

Send birthday, anniversary or holiday cards

Let customers know when more of their favorite items come in

Inform customers of sales

Invite customers to special events

Keeping in touch this way encourages customers to come back to your store more often. **They feel special and valued** — a feeling most people want to feel again and again.

The more the customer comes back, the more they're likely to buy! It's as simple as that.

Chapter 9 Review

→ Why we need to stay in touch with customers

→ Customer data

→ What customer data is

→ Why you need it

→ Preferred customer cards

→ How to get customers to sign up

→ Five things you need to know about customer data

→ Every customer's data is important!

→ Assume the customer will want a preferred customer card

→ Focus on the benefits to sign customers up

→ Assure the customer you'll only be contacting them with relevant offers

→ Make sure customer data is kept confidential and treated with respect

→ How stores use customer data to tether customers

Chapter 10
DO'S AND DON'TS OF G.R.E.A.T. RETAIL SELLING

There are certain absolutes when it comes to selling in the retail environment. I understand there are many gray areas where different approaches will work; however, there are some rules that cannot be broken without leading to disastrous results. Some stores will actually have a charity box for when one of these rules is broken. If you break a rule you have to put money in the charity box!

The Rules

See how many of these you can relate to:

DO *NOT* MISUSE THE PHONE

Obviously any salesperson who answers their cell phone while they are waiting on a customer should be reprimanded, if not fired. I don't care what the excuse is, it is not right. It turns customers off.

When you are waiting on a customer and you receive a phone call on the store phone, the proper procedure is to take a message and call back later. You will make the customer you are waiting on feel more important. Besides, it is the right thing to do.

If, in fact, you are shorthanded and have to answer the telephone, make sure you tell the person on the line that you are working with a customer now and you will call them back at the earliest possible convenience. This goes in the category of "a bird in the hand is worth two in the bush." Focus on the customer you are with.

Not following these rules will result in losing the sale (or certainly any chance of a repeat sale). Along with losing the sale, your credibility and opportunity to build a long-term relationship just went out the window.

TEXTING

There is a **do** and a **don't** here. The **do** is to get involved in a texting service to keep in touch with your customers. It is one of the most powerful tools available to retailers today.

The don't is never text or allow any of your employees to ever text while taking care of a customer. It is the proverbial "kiss of death."

DO *NOT* IMPOSE YOUR OWN WILL/TASTE

Continuing to show an item the customer does not like but the salesperson does comes under the category of "the road to hell is paved with good intentions." Let me explain how this happens. A customer comes in and asks for a specific category of merchandise. You show them item A, item B, and item C. Everyone you've shown these three items to has fallen in love with item A. So, you decide not to bother showing item C to this customer. To make the sale easier and faster, you just show them A and B. Again, everyone else has picked item A. So, you decide not to waste your time with item B, either. You just show item A.

That is working fine until a customer says to you, "I don't like it." In response you say, "But you don't understand! This is the hottest item we have in the store!" And the customer says again, "But I don't like it." Instead of giving up when they say that, you try to show it again, only aggravating the customer further and losing the sale.

Here's what so dangerous about showing only item A: That customer needs a point of reference to begin to understand why they like what they like and why one choice is better than the other. Take away the sense of comparison and you will lose the sale.

Remember: Customers need to have easy choices. It doesn't hurt to show an item they may even hate, because it makes the comparison that much easier for them.

FAILURE TO RE-SUGGEST

This selling **don't** goes along with the point above. Let's say the customer says they don't like an item and they are emphatic about it. The salesperson becomes petrified to show the item the customer just said they hated. They become afraid the customer will chop their head off. The truth is, after they've said they hate something and you've shown them some other items, it becomes appropriate (in fact, it's the perfect time) to re-suggest the initial item.

Doing so will show that you are a pro and you believe in your merchandise. It also shows you understand that what that customer needed was a sense of comparison.

DO *NOT* FOCUS ON ISSUES THAT ARE UNIMPORTANT TO THE CUSTOMER

This has happened to all of us. You have a specific need or want, and you have a stupid salesperson who is telling you about things that are important to them, but definitely not to you. I love when I go shopping for a car and they tell me about all of the wonderful features that are housed under the hood. I automatically get turned off, because I don't care. I have owned one car for almost three years now. I have never looked under the hood once in three years — and have no intentions of ever doing so!

When I'm shopping for a car, I want to know about the stereo system, the navigation system, the leather seats, and how much I am going to save on gasoline. Those are the issues that are important to me.

The "do" counterpart here is to make sure you understand which issues are important to each customer. Understand that saving money cannot be the only deciding factor. Simply ask the customer what is important. Coming from the women's special occasion apparel business, I know that customers may value anything from looking understated and appropriate to spectacular and sexy — not to mention thinner and younger. Think about what's important to a woman who is going to her 25th high school reunion. It's a little different from buying a dress for a funeral or a job interview.

DO *NOT* TALK ABOUT ITEMS THE STORE ONCE CARRIED OR THAT MIGHT BE COMING IN

Don't you hate going into a store and asking for a specific item and the salesperson talks about how they used to carry it or it's coming in next week? But you need it right away!

Why would you want to focus on something you can't sell? If the item is that good, the customer is just going to go online or down the street and buy it and say the heck with you.

USE *IN*CLUSIONARY NOT *EX*CLUSIONARY HUMOR

Exclusionary humor is a major league **don't**. There is nothing (or hardly anything) more annoying than going into a store where the employees are all huddled together, laughing about something. You could swear they are laughing about you. (They're not.) To dispel that impression, all it takes is to share what you are laughing about with the customer. In other words, change exclusionary humor into inclusionary humor. But do be careful. Keep it clean and appropriate!

DO *NOT* PREJUDGE A CUSTOMER

Looking at a customer and knowing how financially well-heeled they are is almost impossible. There is a concept today that is referred to as "stealth wealth." The days of conspicuous consumption are not completely over, but certainly flaunting their financial status is not important to many people. A good example is Steve Jobs, the founder and CEO of Apple and the largest stockholder in Disney, having sold his Pixar Studios to Disney. The man is worth billions, yet his public image is wearing a black turtleneck and a pair of comfortable jeans. That is the same image Jobs presents at stockholders' meetings in front of the world.

The book *The Millionaire Next Door* states that the average millionaire in the United States today drives a five-year-old car and is price-conscious about every purchase they make. The strange part about this situation is that some of the best dressed people driving the newest cars are the ones who don't have nearly as much money as you may think. Sometimes the latest model cars are leased, because it is the least expensive way of maintaining an automobile.

Remember the lesson here: Prejudging can kill potential sales.

AVOID THE DISEASE OF LCR

LCR is Last Customer Residue. This happens when we have that customer from hell, who drives us absolutely crazy, makes unreasonable demands, attacks or insults us, and ruins our day. We have to be polite and professional, but we want to slap them. (We wouldn't do that, of course — but we would love to!) So what do we do? We share the negative residue of that exchange with the next customer who comes in. We dump all of the bad stuff that last customer did to us. As if they care! Trust me, they do not. You are using that customer as your free psychiatrist. You are using them to vent when you say things like, "Can you believe what she said to me?"

Get off the pity pot. It's show time. It's time to focus on the customer in front of you. It is inappropriate (and bad business) to use customers to vent our problems. This encounter is about this customer and their issues, not yours.

DON'T FORGET THE ADD-ON!

Retailers make their money by selling multiple items. The greater the units per transaction, the stronger the retailer is. McDonalds recognizes that the person taking drive-thru orders who suggests an additional is a valuable employee, contributing bonus sales to the company's bottom line.

Remember: offering the add-on is more than a "do." It is a "must do."

DO *NOT* STOP BEFORE THE CUSTOMER IS DONE BUYING

This is similar to forgetting the add-on, but this **don't** scenario can happen after a salesperson has made one or two suggestions of other merchandise and the customer agrees to buy it. But then the retailer stops suggesting items, as if to say, "We're done here. You've bought enough." Shame on that salesperson!

KNOW AND USE THE FOUR MAGIC WORDS OF RETAIL SELLING

Those four words again are: "Did you see this?"

If every retailer would teach their employees the "Did you see this?" rule, their sales performance would improve immediately.

It is a wonderful opening or ice breaker line.

It is the perfect transitional line that segues the customer into the multiple-item sale.

And it is a great closing line, as well. The customer will tell you when they are done by saying "I think I've bought enough!" or something to that effect.

THE MOST IMPORTANT OPENER IN RETAIL SELLING

This amazingly effective phrase is "Tell me about _____." GREAT salespeople, contrary to popular belief, are not the ones doing all the talking in a selling situation. GREAT salespeople will ask short, open-ended questions and wait for the customer to respond in detail. You want to avoid asking closed-ended questions. If the buyer can respond with a simple "yes" or "no" it's not a good question. The goal is to get the customer talking, which breaks down the customer's natural resistance.

Make this part of your regular selling routine. When the buyer says just about anything, you respond with, "Tell me about_____." It gets the customer talking, clarifies their wants and needs, and opens your path to building a relationship with the customer and making the sale.

THE TWO MOST IMPORTANT BENEFIT STATEMENT WORDS: "WHICH MEANS"

The reason these words are so important is because customers buy benefits and not features. Features tell/benefits sell. People buy what will benefit them. A feature on a car might be that it has an 8-cylinder super-duper engine. The associated benefit is you will be driving a car with lots of power.

Features and benefits confuse people all the time. What is a feature and what is a benefit? Many books spend lots of time teaching people the difference, which technically is the right way to learn it. However, in my humble opinion, it is so much easier to tell your sales associates that after they talk about a product they should simply follow it with "which means" because "which means" is the key to unlocking the benefit. Sometimes you have to repeat it a few times.

THE ABSOLUTELY SUPER, SINGLE MOST WONDERFUL WORD IN GREAT RETAIL SELLING

Ha! There isn't one! I wrote that line to demonstrate the power and effectiveness of humor within the selling process. Lighten up and don't take yourself too seriously! Remember that your customers (or most of them) consider shopping a fun activity.

> **Remember: don't take the fun away! Be creative, have fun yourself, and don't be afraid to be a little outrageous!**

Chapter 10 Review

➔ There are certain absolutes when it comes to selling in the retail environment

➔ The Rules

Don't misuse the phone

Texting do's don'ts

Don't impose your own will/taste

Failure to re-suggest

Don't focus on issues that are unimportant to the customer

Do make sure you understand which issues are important to each customer

Don't talk about items the store once carried or that might be coming in

Use inclusionary not exclusionary humor

Don't prejudge a customer

Avoid the disease of LCR (Last Customer Residue)

Don't forget the add-on

Don't stop before the customer is done buying

Know and use the four magic words of retail selling: "Did you see this?"

The most important opener in retail selling: "Tell me about _____."

The two most important benefit statement words: "Which means"

➔ Lighten up and don't take yourself too seriously

➔ Remember that customers consider shopping a fun activity

AFTERWORD

The last chapter in the *King James Bible* is a chapter called "Revelation."

As we conclude this book, hopefully you have had a revelation about retail selling. In this book we have tried to reveal to you what G.R.E.A.T. Retail Selling really means and what it can do for your business.

G.R.E.A.T. Selling is:

An inviting, welcoming greeting.

Researching and asking the customer questions to better service them.

Experimenting and making suggestions that will fulfill the customer's needs and wants while closing the sale.

Remembering the add-on sale to increase the units per transaction.

Tethering customers to your business by reaching out with offers they want to know about, at the appropriate time, and at a price the customer wants to pay.

Take these ideas and concepts and make them your own. Send us your feedback as to how all of these G.R.E.A.T. Selling techniques worked for you. E-mail me anytime at rick@ricksegel.com.

Matthew and I wish you GREAT Selling!

CPSIA information can be obtained at www.ICGtesting.com
Printed in the USA
LVOW05s2158210414

382664LV00011B/193/P